Creating Queens™

Secrets in Pageantry

Suzy Bootz

DEDICATION

This book is dedicated to my husband and soul mate Jason, who encourages me to reach beyond my own expectations and achieve my greatest dreams.

Also to every person who dedicated their time and story towards this book. Each of you are amazing and have contributed your talents and passions towards epitomizing true beauty from the inside out. A special thanks to Joey Retherford of *The Competitive Image* for styling me for the book cover, Clay Spann for my beautiful book cover photographs, hair & maek-up and Lauri Rottmayer for the cover graphic art.

Thank you to all of my queens for allowing me to be a part of your journey. I am inspired by you, in awe of you, and forever grateful for you.

Creating Queens ™. Copyright ©2011 Suzy Bootz. Printed and bound in the United States of America. All rights reserved. No part of this book may be reproduced or transmitted in any form or by any means, electronic or mechanical, including photocopying, recording, or by an information storage and retrieval system – except by a reviewer who may quote brief passages in a review to be printed in a magazine, newspaper, or on the Web – without permission in writing from the publisher. For information please send email inquiry to info@suzybootz.com.

Although the author and publisher have made every effort to ensure the accuracy and completeness of information contained in this book, we assume no responsibility for errors, inaccuracies, omissions, or any inconsistencies contained herein. Any slights of people, places, or organizations are unintentional.

First Printing 2012

ISBN 978-0-615-64267-3

ATTENTION CORPORATIONS, UNIVERSITIES, COLLEGES, AND PROFESSIONAL ORGANIZATIONS: Quantity discounts are available on bulk purchases of this book for educational, gift purposes, or as premiums for increasing magazine subscriptions or renewals. Special book or book excerpts can also be created to fit specific needs. For information, please contact suzy@suzybootz.com.

Table of Contents

DEDICATION	3
PREFACE	9
INTRODUCTION	11
MY STORY	17
UNDERSTANDING YOUR MOTIVATION	*25*
DISCOVERING YOUR "WHY"	27
DISCOVERING YOUR "THEME"	31
THE "COMPLETE PACKAGE"	61
CONNECTING WITH YOUR JUDGES	*69*
WINNING IN JUDGES INTERVIEW	71
PREPARING FOR YOUR JUDGES INTERVIEW	79
KNOW HOW TO HANDLE CONTROVERSIAL QUESTIONS	91
PREPARING FOR THE DECEPTIVE QUESTIONS:	103
SHARING YOURSELF WITH THE JUDGES	109
DEVELOPING YOUR PLATFORM	117
OPENING AND CLOSING STATEMENTS	125
QUESTIONS, QUESTIONS, AND MORE QUESTIONS	133
PRESENTING THE BEST VERSION OF YOURSELF	*153*
CREATING THE STAGE THROUGH THE "THEATRE OF THE MIND"	155
CREATING A WINNING IMAGE	163
MASTERING THE ART OF THE ON-STAGE PRESENTATION	171
USING THE POWER OF YOUR VOICE	177
THE EVENING GOWN COMPETITION	185

THE ART OF THE FACE – PERFECTING YOUR MAKE-UP 189

THE A,B,C'S OF PERFECTING YOUR ONSTAGE PRESENTATION 197

MENTAL CONDITIONING 207

THE WINNING ATTITUDE 217

BEYOND THE CROWN *231*

AFTER THE PAGEANT... 233

BREAST CANCER AWARENESS 239

PREFACE

Thank you for purchasing this book and for your commitment to excellence in pageantry. I would also like to thank all of the contributors who shared their inspirational stories, advice, and left a piece of their journey through pageantry with the many who will be empowered by your words. This book is a snapshot of many of the techniques I have learned and refined, and refined again based on my over 25 years of pageantry and life experiences. Although this book is only a glimpse of the steps through your successful pageant journey, it provides an insight to help you develop a foundation to grow personally, professionally and of course to refine your pageant skill set. Continue sharing your stories and helping to inspire, encourage, and empower those around you. This is what pageantry is meant to be for, and with every step you take towards the crown, you will also help to not only redefine yourself but redefine the world of pageantry.

Intro
i

INTRODUCTION

> *"May your journey through pageantry teach you that a crown does not define you any more than a car, clothing, or your friends do. You are defined by your character, your integrity, and your actions. Pageantry is not a destination... it is a journey."*
>
> Suzy Bootz

Behind every pageant journey there is a story to be told. A tale of inspiration, dedication, and commitment to achieving a dream, and pageantry allows a woman the opportunity to tell her story while challenging herself to become a greater version of who she already is. At some point in our lives, I believe that we have all experienced the desire of wanting something better for ourselves, but not necessarily knowing the proper steps to take in order to help ourselves improve. Within each of us, we have the desire to make a difference and leave a legacy behind of contribution and improvement. I believe that pageantry allows a woman a voice, and an opportunity to empower herself through getting to use her voice to make that difference both in her life as well as in the life of another.

From an outsiders perspective I believe that many people only get to see the very superficial level of pageants. Most of us can recall a time when we sat in front of the television, watching our favorite contestant compete in a pageant, but unless you are a part of the "village" that helps create the queen, few truly understand the sacrifice and dedication it takes to pursue this endeavor. From the world inside of this incredible bond of sisters, there are stories that shake the most grounded person and amaze and inspire those who need it most. I have heard stories of triumph, pain, and perseverance, and I have also met many beautiful women who are struggling to share their story and find purpose in their journey. Without one you cannot reach the other, so this book is intended to bring together the bonds of the sisterhood while offering insight, lessons, and inspiration from those who have managed to reach their pageant goals on all levels.

Whether you are new to pageants or a seasoned contestant, my goal is to continue to inspire, encourage, and empower you into realizing that your journey is never being defined or validated by a crown and banner. Your journey is about celebrating yourself and the person who you have become because of, or in spite of your experiences. In order to enjoy the process of pageantry, you must first understand your motivation for entering any pageant and what you ultimately want to get out of the experience. If you dig beneath the surface you will discover that your soul is creating this experience for you so you may realize that any goal begins with a dream, is executed with a plan, and is validated by you alone and not a panel of judges.

What is your story? What drives you to share your passions and talents with those contestants around you who are touched by your words with every interaction you have? If you realize today that the process of reaching any goal begins and ends with you, then you will discover gifts and characteristics about yourself that you never even knew you possessed. You will learn that you alone are the opinion that matters, the voice that makes a difference in your own life, and the captain of your own ship. Pageantry just serves as the mirror and allows you to see the reflection of yourself at this present moment. It can never define you, because you are always changing, moving forward, and reinventing yourself through the experiences that you have each and every moment of your life. It is just in the celebration of those moments where you get to share yourself with another, and somewhere along the journey, realize that you were always enough.

The journey to the crown begins before you even step foot off of the airplane and onto the stage to compete. Your journey begins at the point when you make a conscious decision to connect with your dream, and turn it into tangible form from your own thoughts, emotions, and actions. This is the stage where you need to celebrate your unique qualities, rather than compromise them to become just like everybody else standing on that stage. When you understand and recognize your strengths and weaknesses, you will be able to strategically improve each to gain the competitive edge over your greatest competitor – yourself.

As a former state, national, and international pageant winner, I can honestly say that I knew before I even walked into the interview room whether or not I was going to win the pageant I had entered. Even through the past seven years of being a pageant coach and producing numerous, my queens have verbally shared the same experience with me prior to their ever walking off the plane and into the competitive arena. They experienced a different feeling; one of ease and peace which ultimately provided them with a greater sense of confidence to be their personal best.

That being said, when contestants enter a pageant, how is it that so much emphasis, time, and resources are expended through purchasing expensive evening gowns, interview suits, photographers, and hair and make-up artists if each of these queens including myself, never even met the judges who will have already placed them in the number one position of winner? If so much time is being spent focusing on the end result of the competition, then what do you think these winners did in preparation before they even walked into the hotel to check into their rooms? In other words, when a pageant is won or lost before you even meet the panel of judges, then what does it take to win a pageant and what ultimately goes into creating the queen?

With so many pageant books being written about how to answer questions, how to win an interview, and how to be knowledgeable about pageantry in general, I wanted to write a book about how to actually *win* a pageant, but most importantly how to realize any goal you desire to experience just through the power of your own ability's. Pageantry is the ultimate lesson in learning how to realize an intangible goal, develop self-esteem and most importantly, self-acceptance. Contestants have a propensity to mimic other successful pageant contestants without really understanding on a very strategic level what the winners are specifically doing to win a pageant and turn their dreams into a reality. Think about it, if you felt from the bottom of your soul that you were going to win a pageant before even boarding the plane to your competition location, wouldn't you compete better and more importantly…what would you do with the title if you knew you had one year to make a difference?

Rather than walking you through a pageant competition from the outside looking in… I am going to take you step by step through the competition so you know from your mind, body, and soul how to *win* a pageant and apply these skills towards anything you desire to accomplish in your life. I am going to teach you how to tap into your spiritual, emotional, and physical best and help you make your dreams come true. You can use these methods to not only compete successfully in pageantry, but you can also apply them to each and every goal you desire to attain and practice them so they become second nature to you.

Accept the challenge to look within yourself in discovering your greatest tools for achievement, and realize that everything you wish for, you have the ability to achieve. The same basic elements of developing your interview skills, platform, and mastering the stage are applied to any competition, but knowing how to apply your skills will set you apart and help you to shine on stage. These pages are filled with the lessons that have proven successful with winners towards gaining the competitive edge, as well as stories that will inspire and encourage you to never give up on your dreams. My hope is that throughout your competitions you never lose that unique ability to stand out among the crowd and celebrate your passions, your joy, and your truth on that stage! Realize that pageants are a "me, myself, and I" sport and you have only yourself to compete against. When you look in the mirror and face your greatest competitor, then you will realize what the true celebration of pageantry is about. I hope to inspire you, encourage you, and ultimately empower you to become your own greatest competitor. At the end of the runway, you will realize that you possessed within yourself the greatest ability to create your life in the exact way you wanted to design it. Through self-acceptance, self-love, and self-sufficiency, you will realize that you hold the power to make all of your dreams come true.

MY STORY

My mom passed away on August 19th, 2004 after a fierce battle with breast cancer. When mom was first diagnosed, she had gone quite some time without getting her mammogram. Although I did not know much about this disease prior to her diagnosis, I remember vividly asking her almost weekly, why she had not gotten her mammogram. Each and every week she would respond that we did not have insurance and that she could not afford the $100 test that we would have to pay in order to get her mammogram. I felt at that time, that through her response there was a sense of fear in her voice and I believe that the fear is what lead to the excuses she would ultimately give me for another year after.

When mom finally decided to get her mammogram, she was diagnosed in the early stages of breast cancer which is the best possible scenario; because this initial stage means that the cancer is localized and has not spread into any other areas of her body. At that point, mom decided to get a lumpectomy, undergo radiation, and chemotherapy to ensure that the cells would not have the opportunity to spread throughout her body. When mom was diagnosed the first time, she took my sister and I on a cruise because she had wanted to visit her home country in Puerto Rico and she said that life was too short not to live it to its fullest. Although we took a wonderful cruise, the dark cloud of mom's diagnosis haunted us and it was difficult to celebrate a vacation that almost seemed doomed to begin with.

Because she had been so diligent about following up on her doctor appointments throughout the years, after 10 years had passed we truly thought that mom was free of ever having to experience another bad day of cancer. I will never forget the day the twin towers were struck by terrorists because just hours after the news that terrorists struck New York City on September 11th, 2001, I received a telephone call from mom telling me that she had just left the doctor's office and her cancer had returned, except this time it came back on her other breast. My heart sank twice that day and after she hung up, I sat on the bed with the telephone on my lap feeling as if the world was beginning to cave in around me once again. Much like she did on her first diagnosis, mom underwent a second lumpectomy on her other breast followed by radiation and chemotherapy. Throughout this process, all I could think about is how could this cancer come back after 10 years of mom being cancer free? I thought that once a person was not diagnosed again with cancer after five years then there would be minimal opportunity to be re-diagnosed. It could have been hopefulness or ignorance, but I believed it nonetheless. For the next year, mom underwent chemotherapy which for the second time made her lose her hair and have to redefine what beauty meant to her. I remember seeing her many times without a hair on her head and thinking to myself how beautiful my mom truly was.

There were many amazing qualities about my mom, as her smile lit up a room and her personality was one that conveyed confidence and approachability all at once. She had a wicked funny sense of humor that one would not expect to see from someone who carried herself with such poise and grace. Her compassion for people went beyond her normal responsibilities as a college professor, as she worked diligently to assist students both inside and outside of the classroom. One of her students who played football for a University she taught Spanish at was having difficulties with his classes...to the point where he was about to lose his scholarship if his grades did not improve. My mom sat with him after class one day, because he was so upset that he literally broke into tears as he expressed his fear and discouragement. He was studying, but could not improve his grades and was at a loss.

My mom asked him to write several paragraphs and read a part of a textbook out loud to her, and she immediately followed up with one of her colleague's because she sensed there may be an underlying issue. After following up on her recommendation, this student was diagnosed with dyslexia and learned how to overcome his reading difficulties. Because of this, he was able to keep his scholarship and remain on the football team, but most importantly he was able to pass his classes and overcome something that had been overlooked for so long. This is just one of the examples of my mom using her compassion to help others.

My mom never wanted to be defined by cancer, and she used every opportunity she had to better herself and teach us through example that you can achieve anything in life that you set your mind to. When she came to the United States with four children and a high school education, mom made it her goal that her daughters graduate from college, because she wanted to ensure that we would have an education and be able to take care of ourselves so our lives would be easier than hers was. By the time she passed away, my mom had achieved her PhD education and was instrumental in getting a new Performing Arts Center at the college she served on as one of the Board of Directors. As an accomplished concert pianist, she was able to perform at the dedication of the building months before she passed away. When she died, my sister donated her grand piano to the fine arts center where I am sure she would be proud to have it being used for others who now dream as big as she once did.

The last battle my mom had with breast cancer came on fast and fierce, and by the time we knew what was happening, it had metastasized throughout her body. Towards the end of her journey, both the cancer and the chemotherapy were exhausting her and she was taking oxygen every day because she was having difficulty breathing. Mom loved to write and she kept a journal accounting her frustrations and experience dealing with this disease. We did not know how sick she was because as a very strong woman, mom would see to it that we did not worry about her, but she was very sick. I remember mom and I having a talk before she passed away, and she looked me in the eye and said that she would never allow cancer to take her and that she would decide when she would die. I think I realized at that point that I was going to lose my mom. Her death was anticipated, but I didn't expect it so suddenly.

Mom and I would talk every evening and I would call her every night when I got home from work and had dinner. The night of August 19th I stood in my living room with my telephone in hand and had a terrible feeling in the pit of my stomach. I couldn't call her. I remember arguing with myself to just pick up the telephone because she was expecting my call, but I looked out the window with a sick feeling that I will never forget, and I did something in that moment that I will regret forever. I set the telephone down without placing the call to mom. That evening, approximately thirty minutes later, I received the call that I had been dreading for 6 months… my mom had just passed. She was talking on the telephone when she suddenly dropped it and only moments later, she passed away. I would never again have the chance to tell mom that I loved her and because of my fear I never got to say good-bye, and that decision to this day, has been the greatest regret of my life.

Dealing with the grief of losing mom was almost unbearable and nobody could have warned me the amount of pain both on a physical and an emotional level that one suffers when they grieve. For the first three months, it literally hurt to breathe and the slightest sounds would hurt my ears, the light would hurt my eyes, and just getting through the day was an accomplishment. I fell into a deep depression that if I had not had the love and support of my husband and my grief counselor, I would have been a bigger mess than I already was. It wasn't for another several years when I would begin competing in pageantry again, except this time it was different.

As time progressed I found it easier to get through the moments and found then that I was getting through the days, the weeks, the months, and finally the years of grieving. At the moment when you realize that you are not struggling to get through the days then you come to realize that you may actually begin to heal again, and time has an amazing way of allowing life to move forward. One night I had the most remarkable dream that began what would be precious moments of being visited by my mom in my dreams. I was standing behind a large velvet curtain with my mom and we were smiling and I felt so happy. It was so real that I remember what it felt like again to be around her energy. The curtains were closed and as I peeked out behind this curtain I realized that I was looking at a stage and was getting ready to walk out into a pageant competition. When I awoke I told my husband about my dream and told him that I think I am supposed to compete in another pageant again. My heart said yes while my brain said no.

As the months progressed I decided to compete in my state pageant for the Mrs. International Pageant. This was the most difficult decision I made, because although I wanted to share my story and help educate women about the importance of early detection, I was terrified that I would have to talk about an experience that took almost two years to heal from. Because I promised myself that I would never again take moments for granted and pass them by just because I was afraid, I entered my state pageant and I won. Once again, I had another dream of my mom and in my dreams she never spoke to me, she just smiled and let me know that she was there by my side. This time mom was standing at the end of a stage and she was holding a robe and a beautiful scepter in her hand. She was smiling at me and waiting for me as I walked towards her, and when I awoke I thought to myself if I actually win this pageant, I will know for certain that these dreams are not my imagination but they are true visits from mom. Before I left to compete for the Mrs. International Pageant, I opened my eyes in the middle of the night and saw a brilliant vision of a crown being formed in front of me and it was shaped with feathers with the longest section in the middle, and the rest descending down from each side of it. I smiled and closed my eyes again, and knew that something magical was about to happen, and two weeks after this vision I was crowned Mrs. International with the same shape crown as I saw in my vision.

I remember standing behind the curtain with the other contestants as we were waiting to walk out for coronation, and my heart sank because I would have given anything to have my mom in the audience watching me. She would have been so proud. Just then my husband walked back to me, kissed me on the cheek and told me that he felt he needed to tell me that the song Ave Maria kept going through his mind and he could not shake it. That was the song that was played at mom's funeral. I knew without a shadow of a doubt, that my mom was standing next to me on that stage and had been a part of my journey all along. This was just the beginning of my dreams with mom's visit, and now I realize that the greatest regret I had turned into moments of grace, because mom wanted me to know that there are no "good-bye's as we still had a journey to share together. Now whenever I am in fear of the unknown or am uncertain of my path, I am visited by mom, and although she does not speak to me, she just smiles and lets me know she has never left my side. As the beauty of life would have it, the miracles that occurred in my life since mom's passing instilled within me a deeper faith in the realization that we are all connected, and that nothing separates us from the love of another– not in life and not even in death.

This is why it was so important for me to write this book, because our journey through pageantry is so much more than it may appear. It reaches beyond the superficial. Your journey can represent healing from a trauma that you may have experienced, or about healing from a moment of regret. Whatever that journey is, and whatever your story represents, you must respect it and not come from a place of judgment. Your journey through pageantry is much like life, where you have a chance to empower yourself and inspire another in the process. Had I not trusted my dreams and listened to my heart, I would have never competed in the Mrs. International Pageant, or become an advocate for breast cancer awareness, nor would I have become a pageant coach, or written these words. My goal with this book is to help you achieve your greatest dream and to realize that every moment in life is a gift, so never take it for granted.

Understanding Your Motivation

Chapter 1

DISCOVERING YOUR "WHY"

Ask anyone who has ever competed in a pageant, why they decided to compete in the first place, and you will get various responses. Some will attribute their desire to compete as a dream come true for them, while others know they have a mission to fulfill and pageantry feels like the perfect opportunity for them to share their passions of giving back to their community. Purpose is such a driving force when it comes to pursuing a goal such as winning a pageant competition, because the emotions of our "why" often get so entangled with our thoughts, that it is difficult not only to decipher our thoughts but it becomes difficult to articulate them into words that will not only make sense to us, but allow a complete stranger to understand as well. After all, if you cannot effectively communicate to a judge the reason you entered your pageant or more importantly, the reason you believe you make the best person for the job, then you have entered that judges interview room completely unprepared.

A Dream Come True:

Many of us have dreamt of wearing a crown and winning a pageant, as we can remember vivid a time in our childhood when we watched beauty pageants on television. The dream of having a beautiful sparkling crown placed on your head and that glamorous banner draped across our shoulder has been a vision that so many of us carry from childhood into adulthood. Even though we are now experiencing the journey as an adult, we still see that vision and dream through the eyes of a child. The reality of this dream is that if you attempt to achieve this goal seeking it through those childhood eyes and emotions, it will always escape your grasp. Why? Because as a child, we view these opportunities as something of "luck" that happens to the prettiest, the most talented, and the most glamorous contestant. When the reality of any competition is that a crown is often won before a contestant even walks into an interview room.

Whenever I tell my queens this, there is always a long pause as they attempt to understand the power of that statement. When I began competing in pageants as an adult, I promised myself that I would win a state, national, and international pageant. I *knew* on a soul level that I had the ability and the will to accomplish this hefty task, so I chose not to share this goal with anyone until I finally accomplished my final goal. Why? Because I knew that this was such a lofty goal, I didn't want anyone else to compromise my faith and my drive to accomplish these three goals. I understood at that time that people will often share their fears and attempt to have another adopt them, rather than support any endeavors that they were not able to accomplish themselves. It is not a malicious act, I believe it is because if one person is not able to climb a mountain, they will spend hours trying to convince you that you can't as well. Rather than sharing your goal to climb the highest mountain, I suggest you share it with someone who has not only climbed that mountain, but encourages others to do so as well. They will be able to share with you the tools that made them successful and want to see you achieve your dreams. How many dreams have been prematurely laid to rest because the dreamer stopped believing in their own ability to climb the mountain? Your dreams never die.... only your ability to believe in them does, so please be cautious who you share your dreams with. They are fragile and have the ability to shatter into millions of tiny pieces that someday you may find yourself unable to restore.

When you know your "why" then you will be able to deflect the fears of those who were not able to achieve their own dreams, and quite possibly you may be the inspiration that was needed for them to believe in their own dreams once again. Identify your goal...create a plan of action....and don't stop until you have accomplished that goal. That is truly the key to winning a pageant or achieving any goal in life that you desire! Keep those dreams very close to your heart and when you have accomplished them, share with those around you how you were able to achieve your goals so you can share your tools of success with those around you. There is no greater gift than inspiring, encouraging, and empowering others to achieving their own personal best. Karma is a beautiful thing....pay it forward!

Why is it important to know your "why?"

- Knowing your goal allows you to create a plan of action that will uncover steps towards achieving your desired outcome.

- If you understand the reason you are competing, then you will not allow another person, director, or coach to dissuade you from your passions.

- You will remain focused with your energy, actions, and will utilize your time to create your plan of achieving your goal rather than allowing yourself to get distracted.

Now that you can take some moments and discover what your primary goal is for competing in your pageant, you need to write it down and take some time each and every day to connect with your goal and take the necessary steps to achieving that goal one step at a time.

Chapter 2

DISCOVERING YOUR "THEME"

Because I have been so blessed to work with amazing women across the world, I have noticed some consistencies with the most popular reasons we compete in pageantry. I have labeled these as themes, and by understanding your theme, you have the opportunity to use pageantry for one of the primary purposed it was designed for...to heal the areas in your life where you felt you were not "enough" and dance your dance on the stage to *celebrate* your feelings rather than compensate for your feelings.

Whatever the reason for your competing they must be your own and they must be authentic, or both your experience and the outcome will not serve in your favor. Because there are several consistent "themes" that many contestants fall into when they enter competitions, I believe that some will overlap with one another. Just as no two people are the same, each of us have similar experiences and ways of processing those experiences. The first step in discovering your "why" is to delve into what is motivating you today so you can decide on a conscious level as to whether your motivation is sincere or if you need to dig a little deeper into your "why" and uncover your truth. By doing this, it will be easier for you to share your story with the judges during the interview competition.

Theme #1:

"I compete in pageantry because I want to be told that I am beautiful."

When I coach my queens I warn them that I am the type of coach that will dig through the "cobwebs" of their minds and try to understand their motivation. Oftentimes they are not even aware of their true motivations or their own "why" for competing. It is so important to be true to yourself, and to understand that you are the only person who can provide yourself the tools to achieve the ultimate goal that you are seeking to experience from the pageant you enter. The only problem, is that oftentimes contestants enter a pageant to win it without understanding what that win actually means. Many contestants can admit that the primary reason they enter a pageant is because they either need to *feel* beautiful or be *told* that they are beautiful. Nobody likes to admit it, but there is always a deep desire to have our insecurities acknowledged and appreciated, even if they are coming from a complete stranger or a group of 5 judges who we will never see again throughout our lives.

I have to remind my queens of this each and every day because when I begin working with you, I will discover what your main reason is for entering your pageant – whether you think you want to share it with me or not. The reason I do this, is because if you can understand your own truth, then you will know what steps you need to take in order to accomplish your ultimate objective. How do you know when your true motivation is to feel beautiful? There is nothing wrong with wanting to dress up, dance across the stage, celebrate your passions, and speak your voice in making a difference with a specific cause. When you make your list of your greatest insecurities, do any of them include your physicality?

What is your favorite physical feature? Why?

If you could change anything about yourself, what would that be?

How many seconds can you stand on the stage without rushing off? What is the most uncomfortable aspect of being on the stage?

When you walk into the interview room, what do you fear the judges will notice about you?

When you did not win your last pageant, what were the first thoughts that crossed your mind? Did you feel you were not fit enough, smart enough, pretty enough, etc...?

_____
_____
_____
_____
_____
_____
_____
_____
_____
_____
_____
_____
_____
_____
_____
_____
_____
_____
_____
_____
_____
_____
_____
_____
_____

Can you stand next to another beautiful woman without worrying that the judges are looking at her instead of you? If they are looking at her... how would you react?

If this is your theme, then really try to understand what your goal is in entering any pageant. Let's face it, if you are not feeling physically beautiful before entering a pageant, then entering a beauty pageant where five complete strangers have just moments to judge you on your beauty, poise, intelligence, articulation, and presence, is not exactly the venue to continue building your self-confidence. Knowing that only one person will win the crown, does not allow you the benefit of feeling beautiful if you are not the chosen one. As a matter of fact, the pendulum often sways the other direction and you end up feeling worse than you did before entering the pageant. I ask my queen's this question: if you stood in a grocery store line and allowed the two people in front of you and the three people behind you to judge your "beauty," would their opinions mean anything to you? When you walked out of the grocery store and knew you would never see them again, how much weight would their opinion matter to you when you are judging your own beauty?

This is what pageant judging consists of – five selected individuals who all have their own definition of beauty, grace, and relevance of platform and who are attempting to judge a group of women in a matter of moments or even seconds. You have probably never met them and will more than likely never see them again, so why would you base your own opinion of self-worth on what a group of complete strangers think about you? If you have a strong sense of confidence prior to stepping foot into the competitive arena, then the opinions of the judges, directors, contestants, and fans will not be as important to you.

Now if you enter the pageant without resolving your own body issues before or during the preparation phase, then you risk possibly losing your own sense of worth, and there is no pageant that is worth this risk. Pageantry is designed to teach you to compete against yourself, but unless you take the time to really understand your own strengths, weaknesses and insecurities, then you will always be searching for the approval from strangers who don't have the validity to validate you – only you can do that for yourself. As you are preparing for your upcoming pageant, mental preparation is just as vital as the physical preparation if not more so. If you somehow get lucky enough to win your pageant while you are feeling less than beautiful, then you will just be a queen who looks in the mirror and fails to see what the judges saw in you.

Nobody else can validate your worth except for you, and if you spend the majority of your time and resources trying to camouflage your inner insecurities through outer adornment, then you will feel like an impostor. Oftentimes the difference between the winner and her court is the intangible "it" factor – that one element of a competitor that you cannot put your finger on, but it is noticeable when she walks into a room and she has a magnetism that draws in a group of strangers…a group of judges. This contestant feels more at ease in her own skin and walks as if she embraces every essence of her truth without apology or hesitation. This is the state of mind every contestant should be in when she enters a pageant. You will notice that nothing I described had to do with the most expensive clothing, photos or make-up artist; rather I described an intangible element that cannot be bought, only earned.

Theme #2:

"I compete in pageantry because I want to be validated."

Since entering the world of pageants, I have realized that behind many beautiful smiles, lies a little girl waiting to fill a "void" that she may believe is missing from her life. Whether this void is material or intangible, there is always a need for any one of us to feel as if we are worthy of achieving our dreams. The need for validation may have been created from our childhood, or something we feel is missing as adults, but either way it is a void that oftentimes we believe pageantry can fill.

I can speak from experience when I tell you that a rhinestone crown and a satin banner does not validate anybody. These are material possessions that in their own right carry a certain amount of worth, but it is the person who wears the crown that brings value to the title – not the other way around. Please re-read this last sentence, because oftentimes in the journey of pageantry, contestants often forget that we bring worth to any goal. You cannot measure your own value on who ultimately gets to walk away with the crown and banner. In the process of competing and allowing our insecurities to surface, we often lose our sense of perspective.

Validation comes from creating a sense of worthiness from within, and once you are able to identify those qualities about yourself that you find worthy, then you will ultimately strengthen those and will feel more comfortable sharing them with a panel of judges who only have minutes to get to know you. Suddenly you will find yourself more at ease during the competition as well as on the stage when you understand what qualities you bring to the crown *before* the competition. When you have a sense of your own strengths you will not feel pressured into wearing a style or color that you know doesn't flatter you just because someone else suggested it to you. Ultimately you will own your journey and remain in control of the process from the time you enter the competition to the time where you are on the final stage.

Theme #3:

"I want to heal from my experience."

As a coach I am continually blessed each and every day that I am allowed to help women of all ages not only develop their platform but assist them in the healing process of discovering their "voice" once again. With more pageants basing a larger emphasis on platform in the interview process, more and more women just by speaking on an issue that they are passionate about. Oftentimes with this comes the challenge of having to deal on an emotional basis, with the effects of abuse, illness, tragedy, and possibly the death of a loved one. It amazes me the strength and courage that these women possess within their spirit to not only heal from their selected cause, but have the desire to share their stories with the world around them and offer words of education, awareness, and healing.

It comes as no surprise that many contestants who compete in pageants are also finding methods to not only cope with their experiences, but to find avenues of resolution in their mind, body, and soul. The wonderful opportunities that pageants provide are endless when it comes to allowing women to step forward in front of the media, their peers, and children. By sharing how through their journey they were able to reach the pinnacle of peace, they can discover new ways of healing and empowerment, but as the healing process goes, there are also many contestants who are still seeking that sense of peace through their experiences in pageantry. Because of this, you must find methods to gain ownership of your emotions and discover ways to not only heal, but through the journey of pageantry be able to share with judges in a short amount of time why this title is important to you and how you can help others through the title you are seeking.

If you are trying to process your experience while competing and have not yet found a sense of "inner peace," then your pageant journey may lead you to experience more insecurity from because neither a group of judges nor a crown and banner will give you the sense of comfort you are searching for. By gaining a sense of healing and emotional strength *before* you step foot into the competitive arena you will be able to harness your thoughts and emotions, and create an action plan that will allow you to connect with others who have dealt with your similar experience while coming from a place of contribution. It comes as no surprise that many contestants are seeking a sense of healing and justification through pageantry, but like validation- what you are seeking is already within you.

Lesson #1 – Discovering Your "Why"

Why do I want to win this pageant?

What is my greatest competitive strength? Why?

What will I do to strengthen my weaknesses?

What is my best physical feature? Why?

What part of my body do I dislike the most? Why?

What necessary steps will I take to improve my physical weaknesses?

What is my "why" – What story do I want to share with the world?

How will I share my story and what can I do to help another who has also experienced this?

How will I feel if I share my story and don't win the pageant?

What do I fear the judges will notice about me when I walk into the interview room?

Do I consider myself beautiful? Why or Why Not?

If my answer was no, then who told me that I was not beautiful? In other words, whose eyes am I seeing myself through...mine or the person who hurt me?

If I could heal one area of my life, what would that be and what would I say to another who may be experiencing the same problem?

If I could write a letter to myself when I felt the least confident in my life, what would I say? What advice and words of healing would I offer to myself knowing what I know now?

_____
_____
_____
_____
_____
_____
_____
_____
_____
_____
_____
_____
_____
_____
_____
_____
_____
_____
_____
_____

Signed, your best friend and biggest fan_____

Chapter 3

THE "COMPLETE PACKAGE"

If you look into any pageant system whether they are looking for a beauty, a strong platform, or a strong interviewer – pageants are all looking for a contestant who possesses strengths in all areas of competition. They are ultimately looking for the "complete package." Oftentimes the winner of a pageant will have the impeccable image, the best communication skills, and be the most marketable for that particular system. When I began competing in pageants in college, the judge's interview portion of the competition was always my strength and while I consistently won the interview portion of the pageant, I would be left standing in line with the remaining contestants in the competition. Why? Because although my strength was interviewing, I failed to perfect the remaining areas of competition that would ultimately make me stand out as the queen – not just the best interviewer.

We are all creatures of habit, and because of this we tend to focus on what we know which tend be our strengths, and avoid our weaknesses because they are uncomfortable. Because of this, I coach my contestants from the inside-out and tell them on the very first session with me that I am going to make them comfortable, being *uncomfortable*. This is my mantra and something they hear during every session, because I need to break any habit they have naturally established which has prevented them from getting the title they have always wanted to experience. I believe it is ultimately the *experience* of winning a pageant we all want, and having the opportunity to open doors into a world of making a difference in ways you have never experienced before. In order to make you the "complete package," you need to think, act, and completely different than you did before, and how you do that is to dissect your thought process and help you own your weaknesses as much as you embrace your strengths.

There are many qualities that collectively, will make one contestant stand out among a group of women in the interview room as well as on the stage. They may be the tangible factors that include a winning image, a confident walk, or effective communication skills. The intangible factors are also as important, as they create that certain "it" factor that some contestants possess when they walk into a room or grace a stage. These intangibles can include a winning attitude, confidence gained through knowing herself, and a sense of inner peace in knowing that with or without the judge's permission, she is going to accomplish the goal she ultimately set out to achieve.

As a contestant you must do your homework and research the specific pageant you are entering. You would not dare to walk into a job interview without knowing everything you could about the company you are applying with. The same due diligence needs to be taken when you invest your energy, time, and resources into competing in any pageant. What image do they convey? How do they promote their titleholders? What do they look for in a queen and what expectations do they have of each of their state and national titleholders? If you research your pageant and understand what motivates the organization, then you will know what qualities you possess that lend to the title, and specifically what the pageant is looking for.

To become the complete package you must be prepared for all phases of competition both on and off the stage. You must develop yourself fully through your physical, emotional, and spiritual development. You must be prepared without being over-rehearsed to the point of detachment or insincerity. As the most competitive contestant you must be confident without being arrogant and humble without being insecure. The best way to create all of these elements into your competitive arsenal is to realize everything you have to offer, and fine tune your skills into becoming the best candidate for the job as titleholder.

Many contestants are not certain how to identify their goals, especially on three dimensions which do include the mind, body, and soul. In order to discover your own truth's about your thoughts and opinions and know where you want to develop yourself and what you ultimately want to become, you must take the time to know yourself before you can allow the judges to know you. If you fail to do this then you will walk into the interview and through life, acting as the person you think *others* want you to be rather than knowing who *you* want to become.

When you envision yourself as a titleholder, what is your ultimate goal? The crown represents an ideal and a vision of what you want to *do* with the title, not who you are. So when preparing yourself for your ultimate pageant goal, have you taken the time to define your role if you win the crown, or are you primarily working on defining your own beauty through winning the crown? This is important for you to identify because the purpose of pageantry is for self-discovery, and you cannot hide behind your physical beauty when there is such an amazing and intelligent person just waiting to be recognized…by you!

Develop, Identify, and manifest your personal goals by making a list and being honest with yourself on what you ultimately want to accomplish through your development then translate that into your journey through the title. This is how you win a pageant with or without the crown being placed on your head. There are no right or wrong answers, so leave out any self-judgment that you may have experienced in the past that has created barriers from allowing you to achieve your greatest goal.

Physical Goals:

What are my physical goals and what is my strategic plan to accomplish them?

Mental Goals:

What are my mental goals, and how do I plan to achieve them? How can I develop my discipline, mental strategy, and educate myself on my platform and the world around me to come from a place of contribution?

_____
_____
_____
_____
_____
_____
_____
_____
_____
_____
_____
_____
_____
_____
_____
_____
_____
_____
_____
_____
_____
_____

Spiritual Goals:

What do I want pageantry to provide me in terms of developing my spiritual awareness? How do I perceive my role in this journey and what can I do to create the outcome I ultimately want to experience?

Connecting with Your Judges

Chapter 4

WINNING IN JUDGES INTERVIEW

In today's competitive pageant arena, it becomes more important to have the communication and articulation skills needed to be a titleholder. Whether you are representing your local pageant or a national and international pageant system, preparation is the key to succeeding in this area of competition. More and more opportunities present titleholders with the chance to speak through various media outlets, collaborate efforts with multi-million dollar sponsors, and create awareness with charities that all depend on how well you communicate with the knowledge and confidence that a titleholder should possess. Whether the pageant you enter scores you on 33% in the judges interview room or 50%, your interviewing skills will enable you to connect with a diverse audience and be an effective marketing tool for the system.

The judges interview is the first area of competition where the judges get to know you on a more personal level than the paperwork you provided them. It is their opportunity to build a rapport with you, and hear how well you articulate your thoughts by responding to spontaneous questions. With this area of competition often being the first phase of the pageant scoring process, this first impression carries with your judges throughout the remainder of the pageant. If you fail to impress them in the interview room then chances are that you will not be memorable onstage enough to pull your scores up where they need to be. On the other hand, if you connect with your judges and are able to be informative and confident, they will be more likely to look for you throughout the remainder of the pageant competition. Because this area of competition is so important, the majority of your time and effort should be spent preparing for this so you can separate yourself immediately from the remaining contestants.

This is the one area of competition where you have the ability to come from the place of contribution and share your passions regarding your platform and making a difference in your community. This is the area where you have to "walk the walk and talk the talk." We are all intuitive beings and judges use their intuition in the interview room to decide whether a contestant is being genuine or if she is just saying what she feels the judges want to hear. This is the area of competition that separates the top contenders for the title from the remaining contestants, and proper preparation and attention to detail must be applied.

Since organization will assist you through your pageant interview preparation as well as platform development, I provide my queens with a pageant notebook that allows them to keep all of their notes and research in one area. This notebook will allow you to keep all of your paperwork together in an organized manner throughout your preparations. You can carry your notebook with you as you travel and keep your thoughts and notes collected without worry that you will lose any important paperwork or miss deadlines with the information that needs to be turned back in to the pageant. In this notebook I include tabs for sections such as:

- Pageant Paperwork
- Interview Preparation
- Platform Research and Development
- Marketing & Appearances
- Questions, Questions, & More Questions
- Travel Information & Packing Tips

Tailor your own notebook to meet your specific preparation needs, but also make it something that you enjoy reviewing. I also include inspirational quotes in my notebooks for my contestants so they will remain motivated and enjoy the process of learning about themselves and the world outside of them. Include dividers that you can insert photos of anything that inspires you, as well as pages where you can include journal entries so you have some amazing memories after the pageant is over. The more individualized you tailor your notebook, the more you will want to open it and prepare in the area of competition that sets the tone and builds the foundation for a great pageant competition. Remember, that it is not about the crown…this journey is about growth and development from a mental, spiritual, and physical level so enjoy the process!

After graduating from college with my Bachelors of Science Degree, I immediately found my passion for the media and developed vital interview skills that would ultimately transcend my career and help me win pageants. For over sixteen years, I literally sold "air." I was an Account Manager for radio stations and sold the commercials that played over the airwaves. Through my career, I was responsible for introducing an audience of my client's product and providing them with enough information and reason why they needed to purchase it in a very short amount of time. Basically I had 30 to 60 seconds to *inform* a group of strangers, give them a *reason* to buy, and finally *sell* them on my client's products. So when I hear contestants concerns that a five minute interview is not long enough to win an interview, I inform them that I learned to do it in approximately thirty to sixty seconds…and so can you!

Let us begin with the basic interviewing skills and then move forward to the more advanced skills and how to apply them to your pageant interview. Practice is the key when it comes to any pageant preparation, and training for the judge's interview is no different. If you are reading questions and answering them in your head, then it does not serve you in preparing effectively for your interview. Practice your answers out loud, stand in front of the mirror so you can see what the judges see, and make every effort to win this segment of the competition whether it counts for a low percentage or the majority of your total pageant scoring. Without proper interview skills, you will not feel comfortable and confident promoting your pageant title and your platform.

In order to move to the more advanced interviewing skills, practice for fifteen minutes daily so it becomes second nature to you and you are gaining confidence while still being able to remain genuine and approachable. When you are practicing your mock interviews, do not answer the judge's question by repeating the question back to them. It shows lack of confidence and that you are trying to buy some time to think about the answer. Allow yourself a moment to pause then answer the question. You want the conversation to be a natural dialogue with the judges and whether you are in the interview room on onstage for the finalist's question, conveying yourself as an articulate speaker who can think on her feet will impress these judges more. If however you are at a loss for words and the heat of the spotlight combined with the panic of just hearing the sound of your own breathing on the stage has taken a toll on your nerves, then it is acceptable to repeat the question.

Keys to a successful Judges Interview:

- Know your contestant bio

- Know your platform and select one that you are genuinely interested in.

- Practice with Mock Interviews

- Visualize yourself in the judge's interview room before the competition.

- Project your voice if you are in a large room.

- Realize that the judges want you to do well.

- Maintain good eye contact.

- Use verbal and non-verbal communication.

- Lead the judges interview through preparation.

- Learn to control nervous gestures.

- Learn to develop your own interview style so you stay genuine and natural in front of the judges.

- Practice in front of a mirror so you see what the judges will see during your interview.

Studying Pageant Questions

I am repeatedly asked by contestants if they should be practicing for their judge's interview with the hundreds of practice questions available to them online or through other resources. Although I also provide mock interview questions for my clients to practice with, I believe that it is vital to prepare for your interview with more substance. If your main focus of training is to learn to respond to questions rather than drive the interview, then you will compete like the majority of contestants who compete in pageantry. Winning the judges interview is so much more than just responding to questions in a limited time frame, and the contestant who is trained to develop her interview skills in a manner of just being reactive, will be the contestant who stands out among the rest.

Gaining the competitive edge in the judge's interview room is not about being reactive and just learning how to answer questions. Rather the key elements to a winning judges interview us about being *proactive* and creating your interview with the judge; not just responding to it. Get a great coach and learn to develop your own interview style so you are not trying to be a replica of all the other contestants who are competing with you. Then you can use the practice interview questions to learn to fill in the rest of your time with the judges.

% Chapter 5

PREPARING FOR YOUR JUDGES INTERVIEW

RESEARCH & DEVELOPMENT:

Before you even step foot into the judges interview room, you should have researched the pageant system that you are competing in with the tools that you have available. With the ability to connect through the social media, visit their website, their Facebook page, and read the reigning queen's blog if she has created one for public view. The more you are aware of the responsibilities that are expected from the titleholder, the more prepared you can be to connect your strengths to the pageants needs. If you can contact the reigning queen or past titleholders, ask them what their year was like and how they would have made it better. See what their most enjoyable moment was, and the one area of being a titleholder they wish someone would have informed them about prior to winning. Ask her what her year has been like and how much travel she experienced, as well as how much of the expenses she received compensation for and how much she covered herself. The more knowledge you have about your particular system, the more comfortable you will be going into the pageant and knowing you can handle from a time commitment and a financial commitment, the responsibilities associated with winning.

If you have the opportunity to speak with the Director, ask them what they liked most about their queens and what they wish could have been better in the relationship. What do they want from their titleholders and how much support or restrictions are associated within the pageant? Some queens are allowed to schedule their own appearances while other systems only allow their queens to work with certain sponsors and organizations that support their pageant throughout the year. Learning as much as you can about the system as well as the directors and sponsors allows you to know how you can fit into the organization and how you can envision yourself growing with their pageant family throughout the year.

As a contestant you should know who the major sponsors are and how the pageant recruits its delegates, because if you win you will be the primary marketing tool for that particular system. By knowing the major contributors in advance, you can better prepare how you will partner with these sponsors and help the pageant gain more throughout your reign. Remember, if you are truly coming from a place of contribution, then you realize that part of your role as the titleholder is to help develop sponsors to build the system and continue to keep it growing financially, as well as through the recruitment of more contestants to assist the state directors involved.

Whether you are competing in your local Miss America preliminary, a state Miss USA pageant, a national Mrs. United States Pageant, or Mrs. International Pageant you have to be as marketable as possible.

On an international level such as with the Mrs. International Pageant – you must consider that all of these organizations rely heavily on their queen to promote the pageant and be a creative and tangible marketing tool. I think so often we as contestants forget that the pageant was not created to celebrate us personally, but to help empower women and connect us in the sisterhood of inspiring and encouraging one another. Knowing this, you as a representative of the pageant you are competing in must see yourself and be able to *sell* yourself as that marketing tool.

How is the Judges Interview Conducted?

Some of the pageants design their judge's interview in front of a panel style, personal interview style, and sometimes conference style interviews. Knowing how to prepare for your particular pageant will allow you the comfort of practicing at home in that specific interview format.

If you are presented with a **panel-style** interview, then the judges will be seated next to one another usually behind a conference table, and you will either be sitting or standing in front of them during the interview process. If you are expected to stand during your interview, then practice at home in the same heels that you will be wearing during the interview process, so you know how to stand and move in those particular heels. Also note if you will be standing behind a podium or directly in front of the judges without a barrier. If you are standing without a podium, then practice walking and addressing each of your judges so you do not stand in a frozen and nervous position during the entire interview. You will want to make the conversation and interaction very comfortable, and through complete preparation in this area you will look very natural in this setting. The benefit of panel judging is that all of the judges get to hear your interview together, so if you present yourself well and are able to think on your feet, then you will impress them all at once.

With **individual** interviews, a contestant will sit down with one judge at a time for her interview, and once her time is done she moves on to the next judge until she has interviewed with the entire panel. What I love most about this style of interview is that you can create a bond and connection on a more personal level than a panel style interview will allow. The dialogue allows you to tailor your message more to their specific questions and have a more natural conversation. With individual interviews, a contestant can use her information that she has acquired through researching the judges, and connect herself to them on a more personal level.

Conference interviews will resemble a press conference and the contestant is usually standing behind a podium facing the "press" while answering questions thrown at her from each of these individuals who are pretending to be reporters. This style of interview is not often used, but a contestant must practice enough where she does not feel intimidated in this environment. If used, this is for a state or national pageant. Whether your judges interview is a panel, individual or conference setting, you will want to practice in the actual type of setting the interview takes place during your mock interviews with your local directors, coaches, and friends so you are as prepared and confident as possible.

Personal Introduction:

Some pageants allow each delegate the opportunity for and introductory statement when they enter the judge's interview room and if you are presented with this chance – then seize it! Know how long your introduction is allowed to be and don't go over that length of time. The introduction is the first impression the judges will get and you must practice it so you are providing relevant information that will allow the judges to know the most important things about you and lead them into wanting to know more. Consider this your thirty second commercial, and with every commercial you want to include strategic information and begin the selling process without being too deliberate… remember, this is an introduction. Within this introductory statement, share with the judges something about yourself that informs them why you are best suited for the job as well as your connection to your cause. Anything that allows them to connect with your platform on a personal level so they want to hear your story before you even take your seat.

If you have done your exercises and prepared your "why," you will be able to take these judges on a journey that shares more than the superficial level and the typical introductions they will be hearing. You will know what drives you, how you want to make a difference, and what you are prepared to do for the system if you are crowned. Even if everyone were to use the same format in their introduction, yours will be different because it is your story shared through your passion and you will present it with compassion, sincerity, and true authentic motives. That alone will begin to interest the judges, so be certain that your introduction is interesting and reveals information about you that can take your interview to the next level.

Know Your Judges:

When you receive your official program book, rather than perusing the remaining contestants you must be strategic and go immediately to the judge's page. Read their bio's and see what information you may be able to search for about them on the internet. What you are searching for is any information that you can use during your own interview to connect with these judges on a personal level. What is their occupation? Where did they attend school? If you can find an element to connect yourself to each and every judge on the panel, then you will feel more at ease and can also put the judges at ease as well. Oftentimes, pageants will use a former titleholder for that system as one of their judges on the panel. With this judge, expect her to ask questions that have to do with your ability to do the job and your motivation for competing. She has a personal investment through time and relationships in that system and wants to ensure that the contestant crowned is the "real deal."

Since it is common practice for contestants to review the judges in the program book, many directors have opted to give their contestants the program book *after* their initial meeting in the interview room. While you are researching your pageant, investigate who has judged their pageant in prior years because you may see a pattern in their selection of judges. Oftentimes pageants will seek out former titleholders and/or their spouses, specialists in the areas of cosmetic surgery, community leaders, and entertainers. The more you know about the pageant system you are competing in, the more you can utilize the information to create your own image and market yourself towards meeting their specific needs. Remember that pageantry is also a business and as such, these pageants gain exposure and sponsors often through the promotion of their state and national titleholders.

Know the Pageant System's "Hot Buttons":

In order to fully understand pageantry as a business, contestants must approach it as a way to have a win-win partnership with their director. As contestants, we view the approach to pageantry as one-dimensional. By this, a contestant will seek out a pageant system she is interested in, and once she decides to enter then the world literally becomes all about her. I cannot begin to tell you how many contestants I have heard express their commitment to making a difference in their platforms and communities, and fail to realize that the pageant world was not created to honor them. Having a title is a dual partnership that allows you to support your director and help drive their business into greater success through promoting and recruiting. Because many contestants fail to realize this, a great deal of their efforts are expended on the wardrobe, photos, hair & make-up, and all of the material competition needs, and fail to spend equal amount of time on the preparation of her strategy and marketing techniques that will ultimately make that first impression of the queen who can not only look the part but get the job done!

It is no surprise that the Miss Universe and Miss USA Pageants are crowning beautiful, elegant, and marketable women who look like models, because the pageant owner also owns a modeling management company in New York. The systems "hot button" is promoting their brand and image through the talented and beautiful women who can also be effective marketing tools. The Mrs. International Pageant is a system for married women who have a strong commitment to a cause or platform that they promote throughout their reign. Because this pageant is about making a difference, they hire a Public

Relations company to promote their queen's throughout the year. By being aware of this, a contestant will understand that her role as the titleholder is to market her platform and be dedicated to her cause. In any event, knowing that every pageant is a business and as a business you must look at your possible job as the titleholder through the eyes of a business person. Look into creative ways of promoting the pageant system that will not only raise awareness throughout your year, but also help them grow financially, because ultimately how successful you are as a queen will in turn help them to become successful as a business and that is what a partnership is all about.

Know your Contestant Bio:

The first impression the judges will receive is from reviewing your application and platform page, so you want to include the most interesting facts about yourself that you enjoy talking about and believe will lend to the role of the titleholder in that specific system. The first rule of your pageant paperwork and interview is not to embellish the truth, and invent the "truth" – in other words, never lie on your paperwork. I live by the law of karma, so if you lie about anything in life then you will undoubtedly attract like people who will treat you with the same lack of respect. If there is something you have not accomplished before filling out your application, then keep it off the application and still make every attempt to accomplish that goal. In the event you do, then you can discuss it in front of the judges during the actual interview. If you don't accomplish it, then you will know it remains on your "contribution list" and you will have something to strive for.

Since judges will often ask contestants questions from their application and bio form then you want to include those educational accomplishments, community service, and personal accomplishments that you are most proud of and that will position you as the best person for the job. Tailor your strengths to the needs of the organization you want to partner with. If you have a love for modeling and are interested in pursuing your passion, then enter a pageant that represents the passions you wish to pursue, rather than competing in a pageant where your primary role would be as a spokesperson and advocate. If you know the pageant emphasizes community service and you have a desire and propensity for volunteering, then bring attention to your community service on the application. Anything you include on your contestant bio needs to be truthful and highlight your greatest assets and accomplishments.

Be sure to type your application prior to submitting it and have several people proof read it for you to ensure there are not any typos or mistakes that will cause the wrong first impression with the judges. Take your time when completing this bio, because what you put on the paperwork is what will lead your interview with the judges and you have the opportunity to begin "controlling" the interview with the information that you provide. It should be well-thought and represent you in the best position for the titleholder who would accomplish the best job if crowned. Your contestant bio will often provide the information to the emcee during your on-stage competition as well, so you want to ensure you have shared interesting and valuable information about yourself that the judges would appreciate hearing.

Chapter 6

KNOW HOW TO HANDLE CONTROVERSIAL QUESTIONS

The primary reason for controversial questions is to see if a delegate can handle these types of uncomfortable questions with the same grace and poise as she can demonstrate during the moments she is sharing her platform and accomplishments. As soon as you win your pageant, you are thrust into the limelight through media appearances, and public speaking. As a representative of that pageant system, you must be ready to handle every type of question with professionalism while not offending your sponsors, directors, or the people who support the system. How many of us can recall the controversy that surrounded a national pageant in 2009 when the California delegate answered a question regarding same-sex marriage laws that created controversy. I don't believe it was the answer she gave, but the delivery in which she presented it that hurt her competitive edge. Knowing how to deliver your answer despite any question you are asked will allow you to voice your own opinion without taking sides to offend the opposing views.

If you are asked a controversial question during a judge's interview, you immediately realize that the person asking the question already has their own point of view so you need to take that aspect into consideration. The judge really does want to know your opinion as well as how you handle yourself in the delivery of it. So if you are asked a controversial question whether you are in the judge's interview room or in a press conference, you must be cognizant of not offending or alienating anyone while sharing your own personal viewpoint. If you can acknowledge the positive side of the topic, include your opinion of the controversial question, and finally end it once again with the positive of acknowledging both sides. By doing this you will learn to be more diplomatic in your communication through many types of circumstances.

When I held my first managerial position at a trendy boutique on my senior year of college, I had to learn to deal with employee issues without offending them and ultimately being able to get my point across, while acknowledging that the employee and myself had opposing views of how she was performing her responsibilities. My District Manager taught me a technique to assist me in dealing with such issues that included complimenting the employee while addressing what we both agreed on that she was doing well, then informing her of the issue or problem I had with her, then finally ending the discussion once again with the compliment. Through this technique, I was able to express tact and diplomacy in a difficult situation while still being able to get my point across without offending my employee. Politicians, parents, and teachers are just a few who use this technique, and now pageant contestants do as well. You can use this technique when answering difficult questions that require tact and diplomacy while addressing the issue at hand. By recognizing that there are two sides to the controversy, a contestant can still provide her opinion and end her answer with diplomacy through acknowledging and respecting both sides of the issue.

In today's economic and political climate, a delegate needs to truly understand her own opinions and why she has that opinion. Also you must really *listen* to the question being asked and hear it with an objective mind and an open heart, because you are not only representing your own beliefs, but the values of the organization who will ultimately be promoting you as their queen. Had the state queen who answered the controversial question actually *listened* to the question mentioned earlier, she may not have been so hasty in her response. The question was during the Miss USA Pageant in 2009, and a judge asked this delegate this question; "Vermont recently became the fourth state to legalize same-sex marriage. Do you think every state should follow suit? Why or why not?" Because she did not *hear* the actual question, she was hasty to interject her personal opinion about same-sex marriage and that was not the specific question that was being asked.

How would you answer this controversial question as the best person for the job that you are applying for?

Open: I understand this is a very sensitive issue because people in lifelong relationships ultimately want to be treated fairly and have the same legal rights.

Opinion: My personal opinion is that the voters throughout this country should have the right to vote within their individual states as to whether they want to legalize same-sex marriage. (Answering the actual question)

Close: But again, I do appreciate and respect both sides of this sensitive issue.

If a question does ask specifically your thoughts on a particular controversial issue, then you want to share your thoughts in the same manner as above by first acknowledging both sides of the issue, stating your answer, then closing with the same respect to both sides of the issue you are being asked about.

Because pageants are addressing more and more controversial topics, especially for the on-stage question, being prepared is the key to knowing how to listen and respond with confidence and grace. We all have our own opinions about controversial topics, but realizing that you are applying for a spokesperson position should remain imbedded in your mind. These controversial questions range from any topic to the war, the new health care reform issue, or even children in beauty pageants. Knowing first what your opinion is then being politically correct in how you share your point of view, will help demonstrate that you can think on your feet and represent a growing business to the best of your ability.

When preparing for your judges interview, keep yourself educated on the issues of the day and understand the topic to the best of your ability so you can formulate an opinion that represents your beliefs but also avoids offending your sponsors, staff, supporters, and your audience. Having a broad knowledge of current events will assist you in developing tact and diplomacy at any given moment whether it is in front of the judge's panel or speaking to a group of reporters.

Lesson #2 - Sample Controversial Questions:

Question #1: *Some countries are still practicing the death penalty as a form of justice. Do you find this acceptable? Why or why not?*

Open:

Opinion:

Close:

Question #2: *Do you believe that HIV testing should be made mandatory? Why or why not?*

Open:

Opinion:

Close:

Question #3: *Should condoms be distributed in public schools? Why or why not?*

Open:

Opinion:

Close:

Question #4: *If somebody offered to pay you $150,000 to pose nude, would you do it? Why or why not?*

Open:

Opinion:

Close:

Question #5: *If your state allowed the medicinal use of marijuana and your doctor prescribed it for you. Would you use it? Why or why not?*

Open:

Opinion:

Close:

Question #6: *President Obama's Healthcare reform has created much controversy. Do you agree his plan will benefit this country or create more issues? Why or why not?*

Open:

_____
_____
_____
_____
_____

Opinion:

_____
_____
_____
_____
_____
_____

Close:

_____
_____
_____
_____
_____
_____
_____

Chapter 7

PREPARING FOR THE DECEPTIVE QUESTIONS:

The role of the pageant judge serves to interview each contestant and select the one person they believe will do the best job. Because the interview process allows a group of strangers to attempt to get to know as much about you as possible, their questions need to be formatted in a manner where they will get you to share your strengths and expose your weaknesses. Deceptive or "trick" questions are designed to save time in the interview process and eliminate the contestants who do not have the strengths that a pageant system is looking for. Nobody is perfect, but they are looking for the one individual who will take the job as titleholder with respect, responsibility, and compassion. In some cases, judges will ask questions that will get you to reveal your best features such as, "what is the greatest strength you bring to this title?" to asking you to reveal your biggest flaw. Since they are being slightly mischievous in how they ask you, a judge may ask you to reveal your biggest weakness. When a question is phrased specifically to reveal your weakness, it will be easier to identify this type of a question and avoid saying anything that would make you look as if you are not prepared for the job.

Deceptive questions are ultimately is designed for you to reveal negative information about yourself so they can interview 50 contestants in a short amount of time and find the best possible person for the job. An example of this could be "what do you believe will be the most difficult part of winning this pageant?" This is phrased much differently than, "tell me your biggest weakness when it comes to this job?" but the root of the question is the same. A contestant who would never reveal that she has no time between her college courses and insecure boyfriend to be an effective queen, may however answer the trick question with, "it would definitely be trying to convince my boyfriend that he has to share his time with me and my new responsibilities."

Another example could be a judge asking a teen contestant, "If I were speaking to your mom right now, what would she say is your worst habit?" She may be more likely to respond by telling this judge that she is constantly late to events, when she would not have been so willing to share this information if she recognized it before providing her answer. Again, listen to the question and take a moment to pause, allow it to register, and answer it honestly and confidently. On this note, if you are one of the contestants who is struggling with her busy schedule or tardiness, please find solutions to these problems *before* competing in the pageant. There are too many contestants who have the desire and the ability to work the title who should not be taking second place to someone who deceived the judges because she did not care enough to be responsible. This is a job you are applying for and with this comes responsibilities and time commitments that if you are not able to provide, then step aside and allow someone else who is willing to put forth the time and effort to represent the system have a chance.

Even a question as simple as asking a contestant what she did to prepare herself for the pageant can be a trick question. If the only areas of competition that a contestant has spent her time and energy on, is collecting her competition clothing, working out endless hours at the gym, and mastering her walk, this could lead a judge to think that she has not taken her role as spokesperson seriously. As a contestant and a judge, I will often ask this question because I want to see the contestant's role in this pageant system through her own eyes. If I ask her point blank what she did to prepare and she does not take me through the process of how she is developing her platform and marketing plan, then a judge may be led to wonder if she is just competing in the pageant for herself rather than to utilize her title to the best of her ability.

Lesson #3 - Practicing Deceptive Questions:

Question #1: *What do you think will be the most difficult thing about winning this pageant?*

Answer:

_____
_____
_____
_____
_____
_____
_____
_____
_____
_____

Question #2: *What weakness do you possess that might prevent you from being a successful queen?*

Answer:

_____
_____
_____
_____
_____
_____
_____

Question #3: (Posed to a Mrs. Contestant) *What is your husband and family's biggest concern about you winning this pageant?*

Answer:

_____
_____
_____
_____
_____
_____
_____
_____
_____
_____

Question #4: (posed for Mrs. Contestants) *What would your husband say is your worst habit?*

Answer:

_____
_____
_____
_____
_____
_____
_____
_____

Question #5: *If you win this pageant, your private life will become exposed in the public through media interviews. What is the one thing you are afraid that might be revealed about you?*

Answer:

_____
_____
_____
_____
_____
_____
_____
_____
_____
_____

Question #6: *What did you do to prepare for this pageant?*

Answer:

_____
_____
_____
_____
_____
_____
_____

Chapter 8

SHARING YOURSELF WITH THE JUDGES

The judge's interview can be one of the most intimidating or the most enjoyable areas of competition throughout a pageant. The difference between a contestant experiencing intimidation or enjoyment comes down to the amount of preparation you are willing to do in advance. I believe that one of the most intimidating aspects of the judge's interview is the element of the unknown. We walk into a room of five complete strangers, and rather than feeling that we are in an equal interaction with them, we belittle our own position and feel they are suddenly better than us and counteract that by acting as if we have something to prove. With this type of attitude, many contestants create a perception of having to either elevate themselves on a superficial level or work too hard at impressing the judges without sharing themselves in the process.

I believe that by coming from a place of contribution, contestants can offset their nerves by focusing on their "why."

The real reason they wanted to put forth the effort to compete in the first place. When I lost my mom to breast cancer in 2004, I went into the judge's interview room from a place of contribution. I had no idea why I had to deal with the years of emotional ups and downs of mom being diagnosed three different times with breast cancer, or the fear of every time the telephone rang, my heart sinking in fear that I would be receiving the worst news. We don't know why we are faced with the traumas in our lives until we have somehow found a place through our own healing to be able to provide love and support to another going through the same journey. The one year of devastation and depression I faced may have allowed me an experience that would later allow me to connect with another woman who was diagnosed, or offer support to the daughter or husband of a woman who just lost her battle to cancer.

I have taken this mind set into the judge's interview room, and in order to know I had a successful interview as a competitor, I needed to know in advance what I wanted to share about my journey and how I wanted to leave each judge something from contribution, in the event our path's never crossed again. My goal is to teach every contestant that in pageantry and in life, you each have a story to share. How you share your story and from what place of contribution will determine whether or not you connect with a complete stranger and leave that individual with knowledge, awareness, or a sense of wanting to donate time and resources to a cause as well. Remember this philosophy before walking into your judge's interview as well as while you are preparing for it.

Your judge's interview should be multi-dimensional and include different aspects about your life, your platform, and your story that will allow the judges enough information to connect with you and *want* you to do well throughout the competition. Knowing enough about yourself and your motivation for competing will help you develop your interview to include the most important components. Most importantly, you must share enough pertinent information that will allow the judges to know what qualifications you have that make you the best person for the job.

Whether you are a Teen, Miss or Mrs. Contestant you will want to share with each and every judge the most important qualifications you have and how they relate to performing your duties as the titleholder. You will also want to share your platform, and your ability to work well within the organization as their team member and marketing tool. If you love fashion and modeling, then enter a pageant that promotes these skills within their organization. If you excel scholastically and enjoy performing arts, then enter a pageant that recognizes those achievements. This allows you to remain authentic to yourself and celebrate those qualities that you have worked so hard at developing.

You will feel more in control of your judge's interview and actually *be* more in control when you decide in advance what dimensions of yourself you want to share with the judges and know how to share them during the three to eight minute interview, depending on the pageant system. The problem arises when contestants do not know what parts of their story to share, and most importantly *how* to share that part of themselves that makes them so unique and sets them apart from the competition.

The problem with pageantry today is that a contestant will study the pageant system that she is entering (as she should) and rather than take those elements of the winner that she can dissect, she sells herself out and becomes an imitation or "cookie cutter" of the reigning queen. When this contestant does not win the pageant, she feels terrible for the loss and more importantly because she failed to be true to herself in the process, she feels twice as bad about herself.

As someone who truly wants you to excel and achieve your dream…the best advice I can give you is to be true to yourself. Trust that the person you are today is good enough to achieve the dream you have now. You do not have to pretend to be someone who you *think* that the judges want you to be – you owe it to yourself to be the person that you have worked all of your life in becoming and perfecting… and yes, you are good enough!

Trust your instincts and believe that you alone are enough, at this very moment to make your dreams come true. You created these dreams, and only you have the ability to accomplish them. Knowing that, you are in control of only three things in this world…your thoughts, your emotions, and your actions. You can control how you think about your ability to compete and what you do to relate your creative ideas to your job…your emotions about what you want to do to help another…and your actions in how you are going to accomplish these tasks.

Know What You Can Control

I believe that you can control only three things in this world...your thoughts, emotions, and actions. As a contestant in any pageant, there are so many things out of your control and for some reason, we try to control all of the external factors that we do not have control over, and we fail to focus on those things we do have control over. You cannot control who the judges are but you can prepare yourself for the judge's interview through your presentation and content. You cannot control *who* your competitors are, but you can control how well you execute your on-stage presentation and your entire performance during the pageant competition. You cannot control who your roommate is, but you can control how much time and energy you spend gossiping about another contestant. You cannot control your height, but you can control your weight and how much time and effort you put forth in the gym into developing a healthy lifestyle. You cannot control your environment, but you can control how you react to it. Focus your intention on those factors that are within your own control, and your pageant experience will be more enjoyable and you will compete with more confidence and ease.

Know Where Your Threshold Begins

One of the beneficial aspects of pageantry is that it allows you a voice to make a difference in the lives of others through your platform. These platforms are considered an area of contribution that you want to support during your reign if you win the title. These areas include connections to organizations which support cancer research and awareness, child abuse prevention, heart and stroke prevention, and many more.

Because contestants are very connected to their personal platform or cause, it may become more difficult to express their platform to a judge without losing composure in the process. The more in control you are of your message and what you want to share about your message, the more impactful your story becomes and the better opportunity you have to actually make a difference in the life of another person. Because of this, you must know where your threshold is when sharing your personal connection to your cause and do not cross that invisible barrier. If a young lady is still dealing with the trauma of surviving a sexual assault and she does not know what areas of her story to share, then she opens herself up to crossing her comfort zone and breaking down in front of the judge and losing her composure. When I lost my mother to breast cancer, my platform became *Breast Cancer Awareness and Early Detection*. Because I needed to share my personal story and connection with each judge on the panel, I had to speak five different times and be able to share my story without losing my composure. It was my greatest fear and my biggest challenge. To be honest, it almost kept me from competing because I was terrified to speak to others about something that was so difficult for me to overcome. I had to practice out loud, what I would share and how I would get my message across without crying. I realized that there was always one specific area of my message that when I began sharing, I would immediately feel my chest growing tighter and my eyes welling with tears. I knew that was my personal threshold and had to learn to share my story without including that area of mom's battle.

In other words, I had to "tighten" my story so I could come from a place of education, awareness, and contribution without allowing the judge to lead me to a place that I knew I could not recover from. I believe that as contestants we have the obligation to share our story and let the judges peek through the window of our souls without allowing them to walk in the front door. My threshold was the barrier between my window and my front door. As you prepare your platform and learn how to share your message, allow yourself to share your story from a place of connection and information without losing your composure in the process.

I work daily with contestants who have to learn how to share their story and oftentimes heal in the process. Even though it has been almost six years since my mother passed away, I still cannot cross my threshold when sharing her story but through the process of sharing her story and educating others, I know that pieces of my heart are healing throughout the process. We are all human and to offer support and encouragement to others from an area in our lives where we suffered some of our greatest pain, is what the journey of pageantry is all about. It needs to be celebrated rather than criticized, and this is the sisterhood that pageantry provides.

Chapter 9

DEVELOPING YOUR PLATFORM

With platform being such an integral part of the judge's interview in some major pageants, it is vital that you spend time on developing your plan for your platform as well as your goal in the event that you are crowned the winner. Selecting your platform can be daunting task, because oftentimes we are either so connected to our own cause that it becomes difficult to emotionally separate from it in order to speak to the judges from a place of education and contribution. On the other hand, platforms can also be challenging because contestants are not connected enough to a cause, or have settled for a cause that they believe they are expected to have in order to successfully compete in the system.

I continually hear from my new clients that they were instructed to change their platforms because it is not the proper platform for the pageant they are entering. Often this advice comes from well-meaning coaches, directors, and friends, but I always question this advice because that contestant is being asked not to be authentic to her cause and to herself. Imagine how a contestant must feel when she is a rape survivor and is told that it will make other women around her uncomfortable if she educates them and offers resources for assistance in the healing process? Yes, the topic of sexual assault is uncomfortable, and so is breast cancer, heart disease, stroke, and so many other platform topics that men and women have to face on a daily basis. But wouldn't you rather have someone tell you they too suffered from a similar experience, and can show you how they were able to heal and empower themselves once again? Wouldn't you want to know that there is a road to recovery that you would not have thought otherwise had you not met an amazing woman who took her painful experience and turned it into her greatest achievement to ensure that through education and support, you did not have to experience it as well?

Heed the advice of those who you feel can assist you and learn to recognize the advice from those who are not in a position to market your platform and help share your story in the process. Oftentimes a delegate is persuaded to change her platform because the individual or group of individuals she is working with are either uncomfortable with her particular platform or simply do not know how to develop a marketing plan for it.

When you finally do select your platform you must know enough about your cause to inform the judges of why it is significant to you and most importantly, why it should be relevant to them. Selling the judges on your platform means allowing these strangers to see your cause through your eyes and know there is a need for your voice to raise awareness about it. It is a three part process that involves educating them, making it important to them, and ultimately selling them. If you are not educated enough on your own cause, then it will be difficult to educate your judges panel, your pageant sisters, and your community.

There is so much involved in this section that I almost need to write a book just about platform development and marketing. But the most essential key to remember while you are preparing your statement and strategy is to be true to yourself, prepare yourself enough through education, and know what qualities you bring to the table as an advocate for your cause. You only have one chance to make a good first impression with the judges, and a pageant that involves platform challenges you to go above and beyond the superficial answers and discover opportunities to make a difference. You just never know if the judge you are speaking to about your cause was the only reason that you were placed in that interview and in the position for competing in the pageant. Honor that role, because whether it is one judge or thousands of people you are meant to educate, each person is as important as the next.

Lesson #4 - Developing Your Platform

What is my platform statement?

_____
_____
_____
_____

Why do I want to promote this platform?

_____
_____
_____
_____
_____
_____
_____
_____
_____
_____
_____
_____
_____
_____

What do I hope to accomplish through speaking to others about this cause?

Is there a national organization that I can work with to promote my platform?

What Organization supports my platform?

_____
_____
_____
_____

Does this organization have chapters in my state or community?

_____
_____

What campaigns are they promoting to raise awareness about this issue?

_____
_____
_____
_____
_____

How can I help this organization spread awareness?

_____
_____
_____
_____
_____
_____

What am I doing now to promote this cause?

How can I take my efforts to the next level?

If I could accomplish anything with this title, what would that be?

Chapter 10

OPENING AND CLOSING STATEMENTS

Since many pageants do not allow a contestant time for an introductory statement, then you will still want to prepare an opening statement or what I refer to it as your "Tell me about yourself" story. In this, you will want to include several dimensions of you just as you do your introductory statement but end your opening statement with the focus of where you want to direct the next question from the judges. Your "tell me about yourself" story is in fact a thirty second commercial about yourself, so ensure that what you share about yourself is reflecting the most important and unique qualities you possess that are pertinent to the job you are applying for. When I work with contestants, a large portion of time is spent developing their opening statement, because just as each contestant is different, each story is different as well.

Coaches serve no greater disservice to contestants when they coach all of their clients in a "cookie cutter" fashion. Since each person is different, then each story should be different as well as how she conveys her message. Of course, the basic interviewing techniques need to be maximized, but the individual characteristics of every contestant should include information about her that makes her *stand out* among her competitors rather than just blend into the pack. If you are standing next to a group of contestants who are saying and speaking in the exact same manner, then suddenly the judges will begin to compare those who are "similar" and find the best contestant out of that group. The contestants who are different and unique then begin to stand out, and as a competitor you want to stand out against the group you are competing with. Notice that I said competing with…not *against*.

Just as your opening statement is important to develop, your closing statement is just as important because it is the last piece of information you share with the judges before you walk away from their table and they put pen to paper to score you. How many pageant interviews have you experienced when your judge will ask you if there is anything else you would like to share with them that is not included on your contestant bio or platform page? It surprises me to hear of the amount of contestants who actually answer with a "no." Oftentimes the reason this occurs is because the contestant did not prepare enough for her judge's interview and decided to "wing" her final impression to the judges.

If you are in a five minute interview with each judge, then you should tailor your introductory statement or your "tell me about yourself" story to be approximately 30 seconds in length.

Your closing statement then comes at the end of the interview which should be anywhere from one minute to thirty seconds as well- depending on when the question was asked. Not preparing for either of these is similar to listening to a commercial where the final fifteen seconds of the interview is silence or "dead air." You expect to hear a strong closing when you listen to a commercial because the advertiser knows they have to "sell" their message in an impactful way so the audience will remember them long after the commercial airs. A closing statement is no different, so be prepared to offer yours as strongly as you prepared your opening statement.

Just like a commercial is structured to include the open which is the section where you inform your audience (your judges) about your product (you) then you and finally sell them (your close), then you have effectively included the most important components of a winning judges interview. Now how you take your story and share your most unique features will determine whether or not you are able to provide the judges as much information about yourself that will allow them to be sold on you and your abilities. Pageantry is a job, and the more prepared you are for the job through developing your skills, the better you will compete.

Before my contestants ever leave their hotel room, I ask each of them to call me and we will review their key elements to their judge's interview. I include this as part of my coaching services because contestants are the most nervous and uncertain just before entering the judge's interview room. If I can review with them the most essential elements they need to share with each judge before walking into the interview room, then when they call me after their judges interview and I ask them if there is anything they wanted to share that they didn't have the chance to…their answer is always "no." If it is yes, then I did not do my job as their coach. My role as their coach is to inspire them, encourage them, and ultimately empower them, so I want to keep them centered before they go into their competition.

Practice your opening and closing statements as you would any element to your competition because the judge's interview is often the first area of competition where you get to meet the judges face to face. You owe it to yourself to be able to understand your motives, express your passions, and sell yourself for the job you are applying for!

What is my Opening Statement or my "Tell Me About Yourself" story?

What is my Closing Statement?

Mock Interview Sessions

When preparing yourself for your upcoming pageant you will want to take advantage of practicing your judges interview techniques in front of a group of mock judges. These can be very beneficial for you as a contestant because they provide you the opportunity to imitate an interview with a group of people who can lend their expertise, and assist you in the development of your interview techniques. When selecting your mock interview panel, they are often comprised of directors, former titleholders, coaches, and friends. When practicing your mock interviews be certain to practice in the environment that you will be participating in during your actual competition.

If you will be taking part in a panel style interview and standing behind a podium for eight minutes, then find a podium or something similar to one and stand behind that podium while answering judge's questions for eight minutes. If you will be participating in a one-on-one personal interview with five judges for five minutes, then have your mock interviews follow the form that your actual interview will take place. Teach your body to stand under stress in heels for eight minutes, or focus on interjecting the same amount of energy on your fifth judge twenty five minutes into the interview as you shared during your first judge when you had the most momentum. Knowing how this interview process will take place and allowing your mind, body, and soul to experience the journey of it *before* your competition, will allow you more confidence and a feeling of control that you may never have gotten the chance to experience.

Practice your natural gifts and allow yourself to develop your greatest strengths into untouchable assets in the pageant arena, and you will never rest on your laurels. Honor your own sense of competitive spirit to perfect that which you pursue and you will know what it is to go beyond the crown and use your greatest assets to make a difference. This is when you begin to realize that the journey towards winning a pageant goes beyond what the judges think of you. It is about what you think of yourself, and how high you raise the bar to excel beyond those limits that you once created. You will begin reaching new boundaries and pushing your beliefs into a realization that you are enough. You won't need another person's permission or approval to become what you have always wanted to be. Remember that the woman defines the title…not the other way around.

Chapter 11

QUESTIONS, QUESTIONS, AND MORE QUESTIONS...

Generic Topics:

1. What makes your state special?

2. Who is the Governor of your state?

3. What is your state flower?

4. What is your state's greatest resource?

5. If you had to describe your state to someone who has never visited – what would you tell them?

6. What advice would you give someone who has never competed in pageantry?

7. Why did you decide to enter this pageant?

8. What qualities do you bring to the title of Miss _____?

9. What is your greatest strength?

10. What is your biggest weakness?

11. How would your friends describe you?

12. What qualities do you feel the titleholder should possess?

13. If you were to win the pageant this weekend? What is the first thing you would do?

14. How do you define success?

15. If you had the choice…would you rather be President or First Lady?

16. Besides your friends, boyfriend, and family…what is the one thing you could not live without and why?

17. Do you think the media creates a negative image of pageantry? Why or why not?

18. How would you use the media to gain exposure for this title or your platform?

19. What do you think is the difference between this pageant and the other systems out there?

20. If you could leave a legacy in this world, what would that be and why?

21. What is the definition of beauty?

22. What obstacle have you overcome and how did you do it?

23. If you could change anything in your life, what would it be and why?

24. Give us an example of how you turned a negative experience into a positive?

25. What is the last book you read and what did you learn from it?

26. If you could choose anyone in history to have lunch with, who would it be and what would you want to ask them?

27. If you could change any experience that happened during this competition, what would it be and why?

28. Do you think we put more emphasis on being famous or being a good role model?

29. What do you look for in a best friend?

30. What defines you as a woman?

31. If you could put one possession of yours into a time capsule, what would it be and why?

32. What has your family taught you?

33. What one thing has society taught you?

34. If you could go back and change one event in history, what would that be and why?

35. Should the government censor information accessible on the internet?

36. Who makes a better friend, a man or a woman and why?

37. Would you compete again in this pageant if you do not win the title tonight?

38. If you knew tomorrow was your last day on earth, how would you spend it?

39. What female athlete do you admire the most and why?

40. If someone were to create a movie about your life, what actress would play the leading role and why?

41. If you had the power to change the course of history as it is being written today, how would you alter it and why?

42. If you had to choose to live your life again as a man or a woman, which would you select and why?

43. Who do you think has it easier, men or women? Why?

44. If you could be rich or smart which would you choose to be? Why?

45. Do we often confuse celebrity over achievement? Why?

46. If there was one thing you wanted to tell us that we didn't ask you in the interview…what would that be?

47. What do you think is the greatest problem facing our society today?

48. If you had to give a 30 second commercial about this pageant, what would that be?

49. What is the one thing about being an adult that you wish you would have been taught in school?

50. Do you think society has a misconception about beauty pageants? If so, what would you say to change that perception?

51. Do you think women today are trying to get ahead by selling their beauty or their brains?

52. If you could be any piece of makeup from your cosmetics bag? What would you be and why?

53. If you could trade places with anyone in *history* who would you trade places with and why?

54. How would you describe the color red to a blind person?

55. How would you describe love to a deaf person using only your body?

56. What is the first thing you will do after the pageant ends tonight?

57. With the technological advancements of the social media today, it has become easier for youth to be the target for cyber bullying. If someone you knew was a victim to this, what would you do?

58. What role do women play in our society?

59. What is one quality that you have learned from your parents that you would like to teach your own children?

60. What is the key to a successful relationship (marriage)?

61. If you could be President of the United States for one day, what issue would you try to resolve?

62. What would you do with your life if there were no limits?

63. What would your response be if during a press conference you were asked if pageants are degrading to women?

64. What do you hope to gain in the pageant outside of winning the title?

65. Preparation or perspiration - which one does it take to win this pageant?

66. On a scale of 1 to 10, how would you rank your beauty and why?

67. What is the best advice you have ever received?

68. What have you learned from competing in previous pageants?

69. Brains, beauty, or personality...which one do you think is most important in a pageant competition?

70. What makes you the most proud about your generation?

71. Where should the media draw the line when determining the public's right to know when it comes to celebrities?

USA Sample Questions –

These are examples of 3- part questions that are used in some state preliminary on-stage interviews. These are designed to help you answer 3 different questions without spending too much time on each answer. Just get comfortable with the process **of** answering more than one question during your possible on-stage interview.

1. If you could have any fictional character as a friend, who would you pick?
2. If you could have any Superpower what would it be and why?
3. With the prevalence of social media outlets such as Twitter, Facebook, and Instagram- are teens putting too much information on display for public view?

1 Is it more important to do the right thing or avoid doing the wrong thing?
2. What is your favorite part of your state?
3. This past year Miss Teen USA Cassidy Wolf received an anonymous email in which the sender claimed to have stolen pictures from the webcam on her home computer then attempted to extort her. Do you feel that your generation is educated enough on Internet safety?

1. If you could only go on three websites for the next month - which would you choose?
2. Would you rather live somewhere where it is always summer or always winter? Why?
3. Do you think that today's youth have good celebrity role models?

1. Which inventor would you nominate as a hero?
2. Would you rather make people look, laugh, or think? Why?
3. Community service is an integral part of society. Many people feel that volunteer hours should be required for graduation while others feel that by requiring these hours, they are no longer volunteering. What are your thoughts?

1. Would you rather give up social media, television, movies, or music for a week?
2. What is your favorite attribute about yourself?
3. In today's society far too few of us take the time to stop and say thank you to those who deserve it? Who would you like to thank tonight and for what?
1. Besides a family member who is the most influential person in your life?
2. What is your favorite family tradition?
3. Some social scientists believe that some beautiful women receive unfair advantages. Others believe that beautiful women are perceived as unintelligent and have to work harder to be taken seriously. So do you believe that beauty is a blessing or a curse and why?

1. Have you done something that is right even though you knew you would get in trouble for it?
2. What do you value most in a friendship and why?

3. With an increasing number of Americans requesting government assistance, do you think that recipients should be drug tested? Why?

1. Who has inspired you as a mentor and why?
2. If someone asked your best friend to describe to- what would she say?
3. Should parents of adopted children tell these children they are adopted?

1. When has not getting what you wanted turned out to be a blessing?
2. Would you rather make a phone call to a friend or a text and why?
3. Of all the ways you can work to improve the lives of other people, what do you feel would be the most fun?

1. What event in the past, present, or future wild you love to experience yourself?
2. If you could have any job in the world what would you want to be?
3. In light of the recent government shutdown many Americans have lost faith in our political leaders. What do you think can be done to restore faith in our elected officials?

1. The United States has historically sent billions of dollars in foreign aid to governments in countries such as Pakistan, Egypt, and Libya. With all the political unrest in these countries, do you feel we should continue providing aide to these governments? Why or why not?
2. Time travel has been a popular subject in Hollywood today. If given the opportunity to travel back in time, where would you go and why?

3. The Federal Family and Medical leave Act provides 12 weeks of unpaid maternity leave for higher up employees. Do you think this leave should be paid? Why or why not?

1. The Supreme Court recently heard oral arguments that may in a case that may overturn a voter backed state constitutional amendment banning the use of affirmative action to determine college admissions. Do you agree or disagree that voters have the right to vote on admission standards for college and universities that are supported by public funds?
2. If you had to choose between love and a career... which would you choose and why?
3. What is more important...life experience or education?

1. Recently the media has provided extensive coverage of the death of Paul Walker, an actor known for his role in the movie Fast and Furious. Walker was killed in a high performance car where speed was a factor. Is the media creating a culture over sensationalizing celebrity deaths instead of those people who have dies making a difference?
2. If you could change any current law, what would it be and why?
3. What is the primary role of a woman in the 21st century and why?

1. Studies indicate that peer pressure it still the number one issue students fact today. What do you think can be done to help teens in this situation today?
2. As you approach the legal voting age, do you plan to register to vote? Why or why not?
3. With teen suicide continuing to climb, how do we do a better job of helping our teens deal with issues today?

1. If you could be a National Spokesperson for one charity, what would that organization be and why?
2. It takes a lot of confidence to walk on stage in a swimsuit in a pageant. What makes you confident enough to walk on stage tonight?
3. Which woman in history do you look up to the most and why?

1. With the continued increase in school shootings, what do you think can be done to make our schools safer today?
2. How would being Miss _____ impact your life?
3. If you had to choose between beauty and brains, which would you pick?

1. Texting and driving results in thousands of accidents a year, some of which lead to death. If someone causes an accident who is texting while driving, should they be held accountable and be convicted of a crime?
2. What do you look most forward to at school?
3. What is the difference between a girl and a woman and which one do you consider yourself right now?

1. Many student athletes look at professional athletes as role models and a source of inspiration. Should professional athletes be tested for performance enhancing drugs? Why or why not?
2. Why are you more qualified for the crown than the other contestants?
3. If you could try out any job for a day what would it be and why?

1. Recently a fundamentalist Islamic group that the Obama administration has labeled a terrorist organization has invaded parts of Iraq and Syria. Do you agree with the President's decision to engage only in airstrikes and

declined to send US Military forces to assist in the fight? Why or why not?
2. What advice would you give to young girls who don't feel as if they fit in?
3. Which is more important, and you can only choose one: being beautiful, being intelligent, or being well-spoken?

1. Recently an armed man forced his way inside the White House. The Secret Service now acknowledges that he could have made it into the family residence. What do you think should be done about this problem?
2. If you could be President for a day, what current laws would you change, or would you propose any brand new ones?
3. With prominent football players being in the media for domestic violence, do you agree or disagree with the NFL's position on corrective action?

1. Recently Hannah Graham, a UVA student went missing in Virginia. What advice would you give to young college age women regarding precautions they should take when walking on campus or out with friends in order to remain safe and not put themselves in a dangerous situation?
2. What makes you mad?
3. If you could go back and give your ten year old self a piece of advice, what would that advice be?

1. With the recent death of Robin Williams more attention has been focused in the media on depression and other mental health issues. Why do you feel mental health is something that we don't talk about openly and what can be done to better reach out to those suffering with mental health issues?
2. Are you a feminist? Why or why not?

3. What is the difference between confidence and arrogance?

1. There has been a sudden increase of illegal immigrant children along the US – Mexico border which has strained available resources to provide care for these unaccompanied children. What action do you feel the US should take against the countries that these children have immigrated from?
2. If someone were visiting your state for the very first time, where is the first place you would take them and why?
3. What is the worst injustice happening in the world today and why?

Platform Related Questions

1. Over the last several years, your platform has gained noticeable recognition. What more can be done to raise awareness and how will you use this title to promote your platform?

2. How will you be the voice for your platform?

3. You can rarely turn on the television without viewing violence whether in the news or primetime programming. Do you believe we as a society, are becoming more apathetic and how can you help prevent domestic violence?

4. What is your platform and how would you bring more attention to it at the titleholder?

5. What words of wisdom would you give to somebody who is suffering with (your platform) and how do you think you can help others with your title?

6. We are a society where many women are juggling to balance career, motherhood, wife and her own ambitions. How would you encourage these women to make time to schedule their mammograms and perform their monthly self-exams?

7. What are some common misconceptions about your platform and what would you do to educate the public about the facts?

8. Many people have preconceived notions about your platform. As the titleholder how would you help educate others about your platform and so they get the attention they need?

9. What steps can people take to prevent your platform and how would you encourage the public to become more involved?

10. As the winner in tonight's pageant, how would you lend your voice to increase research and fundraising opportunities?

11. How would you encourage community support with your platform?

Mrs. Pageant Questions:

1. What is your definition of success?

2. Do you believe that honesty is becoming less important in our culture? Why or why not?

3. What do you feel is the most important quality to be successful in marriage, family, and in life?

4. Do you believe that in today's society, we often confuse celebrity status with achievement?

5. How would you balance family, career, and the role of being titleholder in this pageant?

6. Who do you believe has it easier in today's world, women or men? Why?

7. What is your platform and what have you done to promote it during your state/local reign?

8. What do you feel is the importance of communication in maintaining a successful and honest relationship?

9. How can women today be successful in their roles of mothers, wives, and career women?

10. How have you been able to make a difference in your community and what is your goal if you win this pageant?

11. What do you believe is the most important role of the titleholder?

12. Give us an example of when you turned a negative experience into a positive one?

13. If you do not win the pageant, would you come back and re-compete again next year?

14. If you could be a Superhero - what would your power be? Why?

15. If you could be the President of the United States or the First Lady, which would you choose and why?

16. If you could select any actress to play the leading role of the story of your life, who would you choose and why?

17. What legacy do you want to leave behind with your family and community?

National Organizations

There are so many national and international organizations that a contestant can partner with to promote their platform on any level. Below are just a *few* of these organizations so you can develop ways of reaching more people with your platform and have a successful year as a titleholder.

1. AHA – American Heart Association www.heart.org

2. American Stroke Association - www.strokeassociation.org

3. National Breast Cancer Foundation - www.nationalbreastcancer.org

4. American Cancer Society -www.cancer.org

5. Susan G. Komen for the Cure - www.komen.org

6. Look Good Feel Better Program - www.lookgoodfeelbetter.org

7. National Autism Association - www.nationalautismassociation.org

8. Autism Speaks - www.autismspeaks.org

9. National Humane Society - www.humanesocietynational.org

10. National Multiple Sclerosis Society - www.nationalmssociety.org

11. Character Counts - www.charactercounts.org

12. United Way - www.liveunited.org

13. Soles4Souls - www.sole4souls.org

14. CASA -www.casaforchildren.org

15. RAINN - Rape Abuse and Incest National Network - www.rainn.org

16. Stop it Now! http://www.stopitnow.org

17. MADD - www.madd.org

18. DARE -www.dare.com

19. National Eating Disorders Association - www.nationaleatingdisorders.org

20. Stop Bullying - www.stopbullying.gov

21. National Bullying Prevention Center – PACER www.pacer.org/bullying

22. National Adoption Foundation - www.nafadopt.org

23. National Kidney Foundation - www.kidney.org

24. March of Dimes - www.marchofdimes.com

25. The International Dyslexia Association - www.interdys.org

26. Operation Homefront - www.operationhomefront.net

27. Honor Flight – www.honorflight.org

28.

Presenting the Best Version of Yourself

Chapter 12

CREATING THE STAGE THROUGH THE "THEATRE OF THE MIND"

In the radio industry, there is a saying that we create the "theatre of the mind" through marketing, branding, and how we deliver a message to the audience. If you think about any form of media, you are being told a story through pictures on billboards, messages on the radio, or acting on the television screen. All of the forms of media are transferring messages to you the consumer and what separates the message is *how* it is delivered. Does the message inform you of the product you are trying to sell, are you the consumer interested enough to want more information on this product, and ultimately did the message conveyed "sell" you on the product?

Pageantry is very similar in the way the message is conveyed because you as a contestant are creating a "theater of the mind" when you share your story in the judges interview room, create your winning image, or present yourself on the stage. What your message is and how you convey it then become the primary factors as to whether or not you will accomplish the goal you set out to attain. The presentation is just as important as the message, but because the image is so much easier to approach and develop, the message often gets convoluted or worse; your message gets overlooked completely.

Why is this? As contestants why do we spend so much more time and energy on creating the illusion that we want the world outside of us to perceive, rather than working from the inside out to transform our own misperceptions about ourselves that we have been led to believe? When we are creating the "theatre of the mind," wouldn't it behoove us to actually draw open the theatre curtains and peek behind the stage and acknowledge our own thoughts? Imagine what an incredible judge's interview you would have if you truly felt as fabulous as you are trying to convince the judges that you are? What would you realize about yourself, and moreover, what would you accomplish if you could transform the illusions that do not represent you into the reality of who you really are?

By looking within your own beliefs and discovering the root of where your beliefs were created, you have the ability to change your own perception of self before even meeting your fellow contestants or even the judge's panel. You would be able to realize that the limiting beliefs you have about yourself may actually be someone else's beliefs about themselves, but you just chose to adopt those as your own. If you know first what your beliefs are, then you will know if they are stemmed from lies or from truth. You will be able to decipher what is real and how you can either work to improve upon it or use your truth as your greatest advantage. However in order to know where you can change your thoughts that have created a barrier of challenges to move forward you first have to know they even exist.

When you attempt to understand yourself better, then you grow higher and dream bigger. You make choices from deliberate intention rather than through the patterns of habit that may not serve your greater good. This process will assist you in your pageant journey because you will communicate through the judges interview portion with more confidence and ease, and when you share with these judges why you believe that you are the best person for the job of titleholder, then you will convey that message with sincerity, approachability, and grace.

Throughout my own pageant journey, I have learned that through the process of writing down my thoughts, I am more apt to separate the thought from the emotion and truly understand what I believe and why I believe it. Oftentimes my beliefs were rooted from adopting the beliefs of another who was speaking out of fear or insecurity. Knowing what my truth was as opposed to the lies I had grown to believe have allowed me to either expand on my own truths or replace the lies or illusions with truth. By changing your thoughts you can ultimately change your course through life and become more aware of *how* you are creating your experiences. If you believe before you even step foot on the stage that you are not worthy of the title or that you cannot achieve your goal, then you are absolutely correct and will fail to accomplish that which you have set out to achieve.

To separate truth from illusion and create the perfect "stage," you must write down your thoughts so you can see before you what you actually believe. By making your lists, then you can begin mentally preparing for your upcoming competition months prior to even stepping foot on the stage. In other words, as your own greatest competition you cannot become your own worst enemy. Some of the most successful competitors knew before they even stepped foot on the stage, that they were going to succeed in achieving their pageant goals, and in order for them to process the experience, they had to believe it was possible in the first place.

What lies have you chosen to believe about yourself? These lies can be anything as small as the fact that you do not have the proper experience to win a particular pageant to the larger ones that affect your self-confidence and self-esteem. These are the lies that take you beyond the stage and affect areas of your life outside of pageantry. Believing lies such as the illusion that a crown and beauty pageant define you as a person, or that you are not beautiful enough, smart enough, or talented enough to compete in pageantry, will limit your own performance. Remember that pageantry is a journey and your goal is beyond winning a crown and banner. Knowing this, how can you not be enough of anything to dedicate yourself to achieving the goal you ultimately set out to accomplish? Everything that you need to achieve your true goal is waiting within you to be utilized and developed. Never take another person's opinion of you and make it fact. If there is nothing else you have gotten out of reading this book, then let that truth be yours to own. Remember that pageantry is a journey into self, and in the process of that journey you will discover within yourself the greatest gifts of self-love, self-acceptance, and self-sufficiency. This is your story, so how are you going to write the experiences that fill your pages; with somebody else's words, or with your own?

Write down the truth about yourself that you have discovered throughout your journey in pageantry:

_____
_____
_____
_____
_____
_____
_____
_____
_____
_____
_____
_____
_____
_____
_____
_____
_____
_____
_____
_____
_____
_____
_____
_____
_____
_____
_____
_____

Write down the lies or illusions that you have been led to believe about yourself throughout your life:

Chapter 13

CREATING A WINNING IMAGE

Creating your winning image is as crucial as developing your interview and platform skills, because whether you are competing in a scholarship, platform, or modeling competition, you are still competing in a *beauty* pageant and must be the complete package. While you are getting to learn about yourself through your community service and platform development, also look at your external beauty and what features you have that help you stand out among a group of contestants. Your chance to shine on-stage begins the moment you are standing on the stage with or without the spotlights on you.

Depending on your personality and confidence level, you should develop the image that reflects your personal style, attitude, and most importantly...it should mirror the image of the pageant you are competing in. Some pageants have very distinct images that their titleholders possess, and this is something you will discover in your research portion of selecting your pageant. For instance, the image for Miss America is very different than the image for Miss USA and the image also varies with married women's pageants as well. Knowing what your strengths are while tailoring them to the specific system you are competing in will allow you to maximize your physical features.

Although you are attempting to find the system that works well with your personal style, I caution you not to be a clone or an exact replica of the past titleholders. I see so many contestants competing for pageants that could literally be the recent titleholders sister or twin because she created the exact look the previous titleholder had. Please don't sell yourself short by becoming a version of another person, rather discover those unique features that help you stand out and use those to your competitive advantage.

When I competed in the Mrs. International Pageant, I knew that I had a look that I could use to my advantage and to separate myself from some of the women on-stage. Being Puerto Rican, I have an olive complexion and dark brown hair and my physical features are slightly different as well. I have full lips (which took me most of my adult life to finally grow into) and large brown eyes, so I used my features to separate myself from the competition. I wore my hair straight throughout the pageant, knowing that few women would be comfortable doing this. I also knew that the photogenic competition would be judged throughout the week from the candid photos that the judges would be reviewing later. Knowing this, I planned my wardrobe to include large and chunky jewelry pieces which I designed myself and created a more "fashion forward" style that reflected my personality and sense of style. It paid off in the end, because not only was I awarded the Photogenic Award but was also crowned Mrs. International 2006. It wasn't specifically because of my clothing and image, but I used all of my assets to create the complete package.

As you tailor your image to create a classic, glamorous, or fashion-forward image, be sure that it reflects you and your personality, so you are conveying confidence in front of the judges both in the interview room and on the stage. Lack of confidence is easily spotted and there is nothing worse than competing in a pageant feeling as if you have not walked in completely prepared. Remember that you can control three things – your thoughts, emotions, and actions, and your preparation falls into all three of these areas.

When you are creating your winning image, you want to focus on your wardrobe, both competition and off the stage because the judges will be seeing you when you least expect it. You also want to include hairstyle, make-up, and overall presentation. With so many outstanding designers to choose from in the industry today, there is no reason that you should walk into a pageant looking like less than the queen that you already are!

Wardrobe:

I cannot remember a time in my life when I did not love fashion, and I even earned my Bachelors of Science Degree with an emphasis in Fashion Merchandising & Design. I developed my love for fashion from my mom who was an amazing seamstress and would sew all of her piano competition gowns and hand-bead them with intricate design. Watching mom sewing her gowns would inspire me to one day follow in her footsteps. Whenever I competed in pageants, I either designed or sewed my own competition clothing because I love the art of creating beauty out of textiles and colors. I believe this is why I love the fashion aspect of pageantry so much. It allows contestants the freedom to wear the colors and styles that you love, and make you look like the queen that you are.

Part of the joy of competing in pageantry is the fact that we can dress up and feel like a princess for a week or even a weekend. While selecting your competition wardrobe, there are so many aspects that you must consider but most importantly, you want to always keep in mind the image that you want to convey, while selecting styles that flatter your best features and conceal your imperfections. With so many amazing and talented designers in the industry, it is common to have gowns specifically designed to tailor your specific needs and budget. You can expect to pay in the hundreds to the thousands of dollars when selecting your competition gown, so ensure this is the dress that ultimately makes you look and feel like a queen!

Wardrobe Selection

There are several key elements you want to include when making your choice for your competition wardrobe whether it is your impeccable judge's interview suit to your dazzling swimsuit, and finally your stunning evening gown. Here are just a few factors you want to include when finalizing your selection.

Color:

The colors you select for yourself must first compliment your skin tone and hair color in order to make an amazing first impression. How you wear your colors are just as important as how you wear your dress, so be sure to look at your color choices objectively and with a discerning eye. I have heard all too often that a contestant wants to wear white because it is safe and all of the former winners won wearing the color white. Please don't select a gown color because you think it is what you are supposed to wear...choose your color because it draws out your physical beauty like no other color will.

When I won the my national pageant in 2000, I selected a cobalt blue evening gown that I would have never even selected, had I not watched a young beautiful Latina woman who had similar hair and skin coloring as myself look spectacular on stage with that color. When I won my international pageant in 2006, I wore a white evening gown, not because it felt safe but because I felt beautiful in that color and designed that particular dress myself and had a local seamstress make it for me. Whatever your taste and style is, just ensure that it reflects your definition of beauty so you can grace the stage with confidence and elegance.

There are a few things to consider when selecting the color of your gown – first and foremost, you must love the color you select! You have to feel, act, and believe that you are the winner in that color because ultimately you are "selling" yourself as the queen, so if you do not believe your role, then neither will the judges.

When selecting your wardrobe, consider the element of color psychology that translates through color...

White: The color white is probably the most popular color being worn in pageant gowns today. This color is known to create a feeling of purity, cleanliness, and neutrality. This is probably why it is considered "safe." White is worn by doctors, brides, and usually babies who are being christened, so maybe it is a bit safe, but it is still a beautiful color that wears well on many "looks." In other words...white is Universal.

Black: Just as black and white reflect the yin and the yang, as expected, black is a color that conveys confidence and if you want to convey and sophistication, then this is your color. Black is also often a popular color for on stage because it provides the illusion that the person wearing it is thinner than her body may normally appear.

Yellow: I have to be honest, the first word I uttered was *not* Mommy or Papi (daddy in English) my mom told me that the very first word I spoke was *"amarillo,"* which means *yellow* in Spanish. To this day, I love the color yellow on an evening gown because it truly exemplifies my personality. Yellow is known to be optimistic, joyous, and a positive color. Who can forget Miss Venezuela Dayana Mendoza who would be crowned Miss Universe 2008 in her vibrant and elegant yellow evening gown? She was radiant!

Blue: This is a popular color because blue tends to favor contestants with both light complexion and darker complexions as well. It is a color that denotes trust and dependability. Because blue has so many shades that work well, such as cobalt blue with darker complexions and a pale blue with blonde haired and fair skinned contestants, is why blue is worn so often on stage. Blue creates a sense of one being committed and having a sense of allegiance to those people around them.

Red: This color denotes enthusiasm, confidence, and a sense of wanting to gain attention. I will never put my contestants who have a strong sense of confidence and an assertive personality in this color. Because this color denotes such a sense of strength and confidence, I will try to refrain putting my contestants with strong personality in this color of gown. You risk having female judges be intimidated by a strong contestant wearing this color and with only five judges on your panel, you cannot risk disconnecting with any of them. On the other hand, if a contestant wears this color who is confident and it looks amazing on her, she can easily win over the judges. Miss Universe 2009 Stefania Fernandez is a perfect example of this when she was crowned in a regal red evening gown that accented her dark hair and elegant features.

Green: Because this color connects with the nature all around us, green tends to be known as a color that denotes relaxation, tranquility and peacefulness. When wearing this color, people tend to associate relaxation and tranquility. I absolutely love the green jewel tones such as the emerald green earrings that reflected beauty against face of Angelina Jolie at the Oscars. Use the colors that enhance your beauty rather than detract from it.

Style:

Ensure the style flatters your figure and compliments your assets. The most important criteria must be that the dress is not too long or too short. How many pageants have we watched where a contestant trips on her gown because it was too long for her stature? Do you want to wear a gown with sequins and stones or one that is classic and elegant? Do you feel more elegant in a long and flowing gown or is your taste more refined and constructed? Do you have more of a classic and regal image or do you feel more comfortable in a sophisticated and glamorous style? Whatever style reflects your taste and personality, just be sure that you are comfortable walking in the gown and that it suits your perception of what a queen should look like.

Line:

When selecting an evening gown you want the eye to follow a line from the top of your head to the tip of your toes then back up to your eyes again. It should be a fluid motion that does not get interrupted with ruffles, horizontal or vertical adornments, or anything else that will detract from the contestants face. I believe that so many contestants mistake the evening gown competition with who is wearing the most beautiful gown as opposed to who is the most beautiful contestant wearing the gown. So many distractions can occur when selecting an evening gown, and ultimately you must bring the eye back to the contestant or she gets lost in the gown. If this happens at best, she will win the evening gown competition but will not win the pageant.

Chapter 14

MASTERING THE ART OF THE ON-STAGE PRESENTATION

I have always loved modeling and performing, which is why I danced ballet at such an early age and then moved on to performing onstage for pageantry. There is nothing more exhilarating to me than to get to "dance" onstage during a swimsuit or evening gown competition. I consider this a "dance" because in my mind I am communicating my joy and passion for fashion non-verbally and allowing my body to move as if I were experiencing the joy of the dance. It brings me delight and just sends me in my "happy place." I believe in order to do well with the onstage competition a contestant must love being onstage because confidence and joy is as obvious as fear and intimidation.

When I competed at the Mrs. United States Pageant in 2005, I won the Swimsuit/Fitness award which I was so thrilled about.

That particular award brought me so much excitement, because in a sense I was recognized for doing what I loved - modeling! I still have that trophy displayed among my achievements because of what it represented to me. Pageantry is more than achieving the crown, it is about celebrating what you love and bringing joy to your own journey of celebrating self! This is why so many contestants in pageantry are either models or aspiring models, because these contestants have discovered ways to celebrate their love for modeling and fashion without getting to walk the "catwalk" down the runway at Bryant Park!

Learning how to move on stage is just as important as knowing what you are going to say in a judges interview. You must spend the necessary hours training your body to move and turn, so it ultimately moves in the direction and the speed you want it to during competition when you are nervous and just want to run off the stage! When I teach modeling, just like teaching a winning interview, I watch a contestants walk first and then teach her the techniques. Everybody has their own walk and if I try to change their style to mimic mine, they won't feel comfortable or execute their onstage as effectively or confidently as they should. This too is part of embracing your individuality and personality that you enjoy in pageantry!

Since every contestant is different, then every walk is also different. Some contestants have a bubbly personality that reflects in their walk through a little more bounce and expression in their step, while other contestants have a more sophisticated and fluid walk that graces the stage. While both of these styles are different they can both be winning walks! Whatever your style is, the most important thing to remember is to "tighten" your walk and perfect your own style so you remain true to yourself. Throughout my entire life, I always wanted to be a model and I studied runway shows, modeling competitions on television and anything that would teach me how to walk like a runway model. Because of my informal modeling "lessons" combined with my ballet experience, my walk is more fluid and I would be a hot mess on stage if I tried to change my walk to be bouncy and bubbly. That just isn't my style, so I refined my walk and that is how I would suggest refining your own walk as well. You never want to be a cookie cutter image of another person whether they are the pageant's past titleholders, your coaches, or your sister queens. Celebrate yourself and be courageous enough to believe that your alone are enough.

Swimsuit & Fitness Competition

This is the moment when you can show your personality, your energy, and your confidence in front of the judges so you can have a great deal of fun with this section of competition. All of those hours at the gym come down to 30 seconds on stage, so you want to bring a "performance" that will be memorable and enjoyable to watch - especially for your judges! The more fun you have then the more fun they will have watching you so you want to be aware of how you present yourself in front of them. I often suggest video-taping your walk so you can see what the judges actually see from their eyes. A great trick is to play the tape back in fast forward so you can see if you have excessive use of "fly away" arms or a bounce in your step that may not be as noticeable if you were watching yourself in a normal pace.

There are several amazing tricks that you can use when preparing yourself for this area of competition. Since the swimsuit competition leaves little to no room for forgiveness, then you want to prepare yourself as best as possible by eating healthy and starting an overall healthy lifestyle routine. Seek out a reputable fitness trainer who can help you tone and tighten your body in a healthy manner, so by the time the pageant nears you are not only looking great but feeling healthy inside as well. Study yourself in front of a mirror and see what angles you look best in and how you want to accentuate your features. If you want to make your legs appear longer, or your bottom smaller, there are many tricks and angles that you can use to your advantage to create the best presentation for yourself.

When standing in your swimsuit you want to be sure that you are tightening your abs from your oblique's, rather than just sucking in your stomach to create a hollow and unattractive pose. If you tighten from your obliques then you create a long line and accentuate those abdominal muscles that you have been working so diligently at creating. In the worst case scenario, if you have not gotten into tip-top shape that you were hoping to get into before the pageant, there are tricks that makeup artists can do to create a six-pack for you. There is even a kit called "abs in a box" that you can get through visiting *IT Cosmetics* online.

Whatever you do, you want to ensure that all of your efforts to get into competition shape will be rewarded at the pageant. It is much easier to stay disciplined during your normal workout plans and activities, but when you get to a pageant your routine is interrupted with endless hours of rehearsals, outings, and external factors that cause you to eat out of your healthy regime. Suddenly there are snacks with high calories, high sodium, and if you choose to indulge in these types of foods prior to your competition, all of the work you spend into preparing will be replaced with bloating and sluggishness. Keep your discipline during the pageant and bring some snacks with you such as cans of tuna fish, granola bars, almonds, and foods that you have access to immediately when your hunger strikes that will keep you looking and feeling good. Most importantly though you will want to continue drinking water and keep yourself hydrated. Not only is water beneficial to the appearance of your skin and health but if you become dehydrated, then your body will retain fluid and make you appear bloated and this is not something you want to experience before the swimsuit competition.

To tan or not to tan...I get this question from almost everyone I work with and my answer depends on the image you want to convey. Most of the time, I will suggest getting a spray tan because the harsh stage lights will wash you out, and if you have fairly light skin then it will appear even whiter under the stage lights. I always try to match the image with the contestant, and there have been rare instances where I will discourage a contestant from getting a tan. One contestant in particular was a beautiful middle-eastern contestant who had black hair and light skin. She reminded me of a Persian "Princess Grace," and I wanted her to keep the very classic image that her features already portrayed. Had she chosen to tan her light complexion, the results would have compromised the overall "look" she already had in her favor. In the end our efforts paid off because she won the pageant and remained true to herself throughout the entire journey.

Chapter 15

USING THE POWER OF YOUR VOICE

One of the benefits of having a job in Radio Sales & Marketing was that I had access to incredibly talented on-air talent who knew how to use their voice to gain ratings, sponsorships, and success in their industry. I must admit, there were many times when I was asked to record commercials for clients when they needed a female voice and I was the only one available at that time. I literally went into the recording studio kicking and screaming that "there must be at least one talented female in this darned radio station who you can use for this commercial, remember I sell **air** for a living!" Despite my repetitive avoidance techniques, they ultimately found me and I had to learn how to use my voice in order to help our clients radio spots be successful. In one particular instance when I first began my job in radio, one of the jocks asked me to record a commercial for a national insurance company. After he placed the microphone two inches from my frozen face, he instructed me to relax and just speak "normally." Once I recorded the commercial I looked over at him in relief and although hoping for a compliment, his response was as follows; "Thank you

Suzy, now let's try this again and this time...maybe you can sound as if you actually have a *pulse*." Really?!

I remember his comment so vividly because although I thought that I was speaking *naturally*, my nerves got the best of me, and as a result my throat became tight and my tone became very monotone. This often happens to contestants when we walk into the judge's interview room, because extreme nervousness and tension results in our natural conversational tone to be replaced with lack of influx and a monotone sound. When you practice your mock interview questions, you must speak out loud and hear yourself responding to the questions so you can rehearse using your voice to your advantage. Practicing your questions in your head is like a dancer practicing her routine in her head and not training her muscles to move in the direction that she wants her body to flow.

An effective tool in practicing your judge's interview is to record your own answers and listen to how your influx and tone is when you are answering your questions. You need to hear what the judges hear and see what the judges see, and a recorder is very accessible through your own telephone apps, or using a small handheld recorder that fits into your purse will allow you the freedom of practicing control over your voice when you are nervous. One of the tricks of the trade I was taught in the radio industry was that before I had to do a read for a commercial I needed to read out loud, the commercial script in the highest pitch that my voice could muster. After I finished reading it in the highest pitch, then I had to read the script in the lowest tone my voice could attain. This exercise allowed my voice to relax enough that once the microphone was placed in front of me, I would still sound natural and appealing to the audience I was trying to reach. If you can practice this as you are preparing for your mock interviews, and again before you go down to your judges interview room then you will sound more natural and sincere during the interview process.

Tips to Maximizing Your Voice

- Take a deep breath before entering the judge's interview room so you can relax your throat and have a more natural tone.

- Force yourself to speak slowly so you can counteract nerves that will create a sense of nervousness in your dialogue.

- If you are naturally a soft-spoken person, force yourself to project from your diaphragm when you are practicing your mock interviews.

- Record yourself during your practice interview sessions so you hear what the judges hear.

- End your sentence with confidence and strength rather than allowing your voice to fade out.

- If you have a strong accent, you want to speak slowly to ensure that the judges understand your message.

- Imitate the professional voices that you connect with on television or radio.

- Practice your interview out loud so you are training your voice to do what your brain wants it to do while you are experiencing stress during a personal or onstage interview.

🗝 Be sure you are using proper grammar and enunciate all of your words, especially the ones you are using to emphasize a point.

Know How to Use Your Body Language

The human body contains more than 700 muscles but strangely enough, very few of them are used when contestants present themselves in front of the judges. Just as the voice can suddenly become tense and monotone, our body often adapts to stress in the same manner – we tighten our facial muscles and forget that the mouth is not the only working part of our body. So much of the communication process is non-verbal, and in order to express your sincerity and confidence, you must utilize your non-verbal communication to connect with your judge's panel so you appear natural and approachable.

Contestants often spend countless hours of preparation on their interview content that you may forget to practice your gestures which are just as important. Remember the saying, "actions speak louder than words," and in the interview room this is also true. When sharing your thoughts, platform, and story in the judge's interview room, your body language can add enthusiasm and conviction when used properly. Here are some key techniques to help you improve your communication skills with the judges:

- Eye contact – this allows you to display confidence from the moment you walk into the interview room as well as on-stage. Don't just stare blankly at the judges, use your eye contact to connect with your judge's panel.

- Smile – we all know that smiling is contagious and by smiling throughout the competition, you exude warmth and sincerity as well as confidence and ease.

- Use your shoulders to lean into the judges when appropriate and your head movements to convey compassion and enthusiasm.

- Avoid distracting mannerisms such as fidgeting, biting your lip, or shaking your foot while in the interview room.

- Make your gestures as a tool of emphasizing your point rather than being too distracting. Follow through with your hand gestures because half-hearted gestures look insincere.

- Focus on your message and in being in the moment, and you will be more convincing and remain true to your own story and personality. Be authentic!

- Don't talk with your hands but use them to emphasize important parts of your dialogue. Position your arms so they do not cover your face or become the focal point of your conversation. Watch your favorite television anchor person and mimic their presentation.

Chapter 16

THE EVENING GOWN COMPETITION

I absolutely love the evening gown competition because it allows women to grace the stage and not only look like a queen but have the chance to *feel* like a queen in all its regal and royal appeal. This area of pageantry is where style, poise, grace, and carriage all combine to create the winning walk, so the best advice I can ever give any contestant while she is on the stage is to take your time! Literally the difference between winners and those who come in behind her is oftentimes the amount of time on stage. This is so much easier said than done, because as contestants we allow our adrenaline to take over our walk and what we consider to be a slow walk is oftentimes in fact a brisk walk in our heels across the stage. In order to present the best possible image of yourself in your gown, you want to consider several factors:

- Know where your dress hemline and train are before you begin walking. How many times have we held our breath as we watch contestants grace the stage with one heel tucked underneath her beaded gown? Before you take a step, you will want to position your feet and be certain both are fully planted on the stage without any possibility of dragging your hemline or train underneath your heels. To ensure there is no opportunity to trip, you will want to check your hem length and ensure that your gown is not too long. Also practice walking in your gown if you have a train and know how to turn, as with trains you will want to practice a circle turn.

- If you are going to place your hand on your hips when you are paused, slowly begin raising your hand to your hip so when you pose, your hand transitioned gracefully with one fluid movement. Do not place your hands on hips while walking as it breaks the line you have created and stops the eyes at the hips. Only place your hand on your hips when you are paused and posing in front of the judges.

- Allow your arms to move gracefully with your body. All too often a contestant will be uncomfortable in evening gowns and five inch heels because it is not natural for most of us. Because of this many contestants will carry their stress in their arms or hands, and a result of this is that the arms will become stiff and not move naturally when you walk. To ensure that you do not risk ruining your gown as you are walking, you can practice daily in your heels and watch yourself in the mirror or record yourself so you can see what the judges see.

- Do not get shown up by your gown! If you have a flowing piece of material or a train that you would like to have as a part of your presentation, ensure that it does not detract from you – the contestant. There is a difference between modeling a beautiful gown that a designer is showcasing in their fashion show and modeling a beautiful gown on stage. If you carry the flowing piece or play with it while modeling, this oftentimes draws attention away from you and places the judges focus on your gown. Remember that your judges are not selecting the winner through the best gown, as this is where the evening gown winner is acknowledged. The winner of the pageant is oftentimes the contestant who strategically kept the judges attention on her the entire time through her verbal and non-verbal communication. You want to be memorable and not just wear a memorable evening gown.

- Glide across the stage instead of bouncing, as you want to convey the image of a queen. To prevent your walk from being bouncy, take shorter steps. When I prepare contestants for this phase of competition, I tell them that everything needs to be strategic so it comes across as being spontaneous. When the judges look at a contestant on stage during the evening gown competition, you want the judges to see you and think that the only thing missing is the crown!

- Take your time and do not follow the pace of the music, as the evening gown competition music tends to either be more contemporary and upbeat or very slow. Either way you will want to control your walk and think about what you are doing *during* the competition so your nerves do not get the best of you. By being present in the moment of each competition you enjoy the experience more, and the joy will translate through your eyes and smile thus making you appear as the sincere person you are.

Chapter 17

THE ART OF THE FACE – PERFECTING YOUR MAKE-UP

One of the beautiful aspects of pageantry is that so many people can create the "village" of support to titleholders when they are preparing for their upcoming competition. If you have access to a talented hair & make-up artist and feel it will soothe your nerves to utilize their services during your pageant, then I would encourage you to do so. Keep in mind that these talented individuals are in high demand, and will usually take up to three contestants throughout the pageant to create their winning hair and make-up looks. If you are the first contestant to book with a particular make-up artist, then you will get the first option for the best time and if you are the last one, then prepare to get your hair and make-up done as early as 5:00am – depending on when your pageant activities begin.

Whether you use one of these amazing artists or opt to do your own, I still encourage you to practice your make-up technique along with your hair before you leave for the pageant.

You have to learn to be self-sufficient in the event that you win, you will not have an entourage following you around to ensure that you are picture perfect for your appearances throughout the year. Many pageants will not allow make-up and hair artists anywhere near the contestants during pageant weekend, so contestants have learned to get their "look" created by the team early in the morning prior to the beginning of the pageant, and not wash their face or hair until the next day when the pageant is over. It may sound drastic, but it works and the contestants have learned to touch up their make-up because they booked hair and make-up lessons from these artists in advance so they know how to re- create their winning look.

While learning to create and perfect your make-up technique, there are several options that you have to learn in order in know basic make-up application, and often professional make-up artists will teach you through group or individual sessions, how to create your pageant look. If you can book these artists in advance, then you will have months to perfect your look, and just like everything you are learning in pageantry…it comes down to practice, practice, practice. Do not wait until two weeks prior to the pageant to learn how to apply your make-up and style your hair, because you will need to practice on yourself in front of a mirror and the proper lighting.

With the techniques being taught in the industry, a contestant can turn her pretty look into a glamorous starlet through proper make-up application. The key is to not look "made up" but to enhance your natural features. Of course, the amount of make-up will differ from the judge's interview room where you are only two feet from the judges face, as opposed to on-stage when you are standing behind bright theatre lights.

When applying daytime make-up it is wise to utilize daylight, so you can check for any demarcations from lack of blending or any other imperfections from your make-up application.

Shading & Highlighting

Using contouring and highlighting techniques with your makeup application allows a contestant to add definition to her features and dimension to her face. Stage lights can make contestants appear "washed out" if they don't have enough color on their face, so when you want to apply stage makeup it isn't about applying *more* makeup as much as it is applying *darker* makeup. It is suggested that contestants use often maximize features they want to accentuate or minimize those they don't. When you highlight your features, you create an illusion of bringing them forward, such as the apples of your cheek, under your brow bone, under the eye, and around the corners of the mouth. When you contour or shade areas, the intention is to recede them in areas such as the hollows of your cheek, along the sides of your nose, or under your chin. Practice this technique if you are going to do your own makeup application, or have a professional makeup artist teach you these skills so you can perfect them on your own.

It is suggested that a contestant use a foundation for onstage that is two shades darker than her skin tone so her coloring will not be washed out onstage. By creating dimension on your face through the proper use of foundations and different shades, you can accentuate your greatest features and keep the judges eyes on you! As you are applying makeup you want to ensure that you have proper lighting on both sides of your face for equal application. The most important thing to remember as you are applying your makeup is to blend! If you apply your foundation and color in a circular motion, then you prevent creating lines on your face and softening your overall look.

Focus on the Eye

Throughout your competition, the most important thing to remember when you are selecting your wardrobe, creating a winning image, developing your interview techniques, and getting your photographs taken, is that the most important tool you have to sell yourself are your eyes. They will captivate your judges while sharing your story and communicate with them during the pageant competitions that you cannot actually speak to them. When I assist my contestants during their wardrobe selection, I tell them that the judges eyes have to begin with the connection of their own eyes, then follow the line of the evening gown down to their feet and directly back to their eyes again. If your judges get distracted with your gown of choice, then their eyes stop there which means that you cannot connect with them once again before they place their pen to paper and score you. I cannot emphasize enough how important it is to keep the connection with these judges throughout the competition that you first established in your judges interview.

Because the eyes are truly the focal point, then the attention to creating a beautiful and dramatic look is about layering the eye makeup. This will create a multi-dimensional look so the colors will accentuate one another without creating a heavy "made-up" look. Also, I believe in applying false eye lashes for both the judge's interview and for on-stage competition to draw more attention to the eye. You may want to wear individual lashes for a more natural look during your judge's interview, but because you are keeping their attention on your face during the dialogue then maximize your beauty and emphasize your eyes!

Smile, Smile, Smile

What is a beautiful smile without proper color and gloss on your lovely lips? If you do not normally wear a lip liner, then you will want to begin practicing because lip liners add definition to your smile as well as dimension. Like the eye shadow, you can use two different colored lip liners that complement each another to add dimension to your smile and make it "pop." I like to wear a nude liner first, then apply the lip color and add a different lip liner color over the lipstick. I learned this makeup technique from Clay Spann, who is an amazing makeup artist. After you apply those colors to your lips, then you will want to add the final touch which is an amazing touch of gloss. Always wear gloss, especially onstage because you want your smile to be one of your focal points.

Be Impeccable

The most important piece of advice I can share when creating your winning image is to be impeccable. Perfect the tiny details of your competitive strategy by taking control of those things that you have the ability to control. These include:

- Wardrobe style, color, and fit (includes length)

- When styling your hair, allow it to move and flow with you while walking onstage. You appear more approachable and naturally beautiful.

- Makeup and overall appearance.

- State Costumes- ensuring they are presented with taste and flattering style to fit the image of the pageant.

- Be the best version of yourself and reinvent the "look" for the winner every year. The pageant is not waiting for you to fit a certain mold, they are waiting for a contestant to *recreate* the mold every year.

- Control your thoughts, emotions, and actions and you will feel the most confident during competition!

Chapter 18

THE A,B,C'S OF PERFECTING YOUR ONSTAGE PRESENTATION

Attitude!

Every top model or contestant who graces the stage possesses a certain attitude and she is comfortable showing it onstage. If you walk out onto the stage without thinking about an attitude you will appear bored and detached from the experience. However if you are thinking consciously about something that creates an "attitude of confidence and poise, then your body movement and eyes will reflect that as well. Often what separates the good models from the great models is attitude!

Body:

We spend endless hours in the gym preparing our body to be in pageant-ready shape, so be proud and confident of what you have accomplished by feeling confident! Take your time onstage and use the angles that reveal your six-pack that you earned from hours at the gym and practice those poses that show off your body while appearing natural and confident.

Control:

Once we step on to a stage to perform, the only thing we feel are the hot stage lights and we are blinded by the lights in our eyes. Suddenly we become acutely aware of our heart beating against our chest and the breaths our lungs are taking. If you have not practiced control of your arms, turns, poses, and speed, then there will be a moment when adrenaline will take over and you will practically *run* off the stage. Don't be a runner! You have worked too hard and you need to spend those extra moments on stage so the judges will connect with you and be able to score you properly.

Drama:

This is the only time I like drama during a pageant! Drama can be conveyed through your eyes and your body movements, so again practice in front of a mirror to see what the judges will be seeing. Use facial expressions so your smile is not frozen onto your face in an unnatural manner. You can also use muscle tension throughout your body while posing in front of the judges to help create dramatic poses.

Entertain:

A large part of why many contestants compete in pageants is because we love to entertain others and doing what you love spreads excitement to those watching. The onstage portion of the pageant is the only time the judges will get to be entertained by you, so put your best foot forward. Smile and present good eye contact with the judges as well as with the audience. The more you enjoy yourself, the more your enthusiasm will show and in turn the judges and audience will enjoy your performance as well!

Facial Expressions:

It is said that over 90% of human communication is non-verbal and learning how to use your facial expressions onstage to communicate with the judges and audience is crucial. Practice various facial expressions when perfecting your walk, and I often instruct contestants to have several different facial expressions they want to use during their swimsuit or evening gown competitions.

Grace:

It doesn't matter whether you are conveying an attitude of Diva, Drama, Model, or Bubbly, the ultimate necessity in creating a winning onstage presentation is being graceful. By exuding grace in your carriage and modeling or by being eloquent when answering your onstage finalist question - grace is the separation between being conveyed as the queen or her court.

Hips:

When contestants watch models on the runway, they learn to place their hips forward and slink into their poses which can create the emphasis on the hips and shorten a contestant by several inches. In pageantry there is often the contestant line-up so you want to appear taller and leaner standing next to another contestant. The best way to accomplish this is to pull your hips back behind the torso rather than in front of you. This will allow you to take advantage of your height and also give your body the appearance of being more slender.

Image:

Just as it is important to present a certain image in the judges interview, you want to follow through and convey that image and take it to the next level onstage. Remember this is a performance, so if you are exuding a bubbly image in the interview room you want to execute that same image on the stage so you don't confuse the judges and make them question your authenticity. Remember that there is no right or wrong image you just need to show your image and be comfortable in your own skin. After all, this is what pageantry is all about - celebrating yourself and the expression of the complete you!

Judging:

Having knowledge of what the judge's criteria is based on during your onstage presentation is important for you to know, so you can present the best qualities to the judges. Whether you are being judged for evening gown, swimsuit, or opening number, there is a general tendency for the judges to look for modeling criteria such as poise, walking, and posture. How comfortable you are onstage and your eye contact conveys both confidence and charisma.

Knowledge:

How many of us have heard all too often the term "Knowledge is power?" and I believe that in everything you set forth to accomplish in life, including pageantry. The more you know where your body is and the more understanding you have of what angles work best for your body type, you will be able to convey the image and the confidence of a pageant winner!

Legs:

Since pageant modeling and runway modeling tend to be slightly different, you will notice many models walk with an extension of long strides with their hips forward, but by keeping your steps shorter and changing the placement of your hips you will be able to take more time on stage, have a graceful and natural walk, and be more in control of your spins and poses.

Movement:

It is natural for the eyes to be drawn to movement and how you move on the stage will either capture the judges attention or have them focus on another contestant. Your movement can be subtle and when you are waiting your place on stage, you want to keep a soft and fluid movement so even while another contestant has the center stage, the judges eyes will be drawn back to you.

Natural:

Execute your movements as naturally as possible, and combined with your facial expressions and overall body language you will "wow" the judges! There is nothing more disappointing than watching a beautiful contestant onstage who is trying too hard to impress the judges, that her movement is unnatural and artificial.

Orientation of Body:

Knowing where to place your legs and how to create the six-pack on stage often depends on how a contestant orients her body. You want to have complete control of your arms which tend to be the first to carry tension. I call these "flyaway arms" and by knowing how you walk under stress and on heels will allow you to remain in control of your body and execute every movement and turn flawlessly.

Pace:

During the swimsuit or fitness portion of the competition, the music playing in the background is often an upbeat tempo that is fast paced. Many contestants make the attempt to keep up with the music playing, while walking in heels, and wearing a swimsuit. This can create an almost chaotic and very ungraceful presentation, so you want to time your pace onstage so you are not walking too fast or too slow. Remember, this is your only time on the stage and in front of the judges, so you control the pace!

Queen:

This may seem like the obvious, but often when contestants are onstage they attempt to emulate supermodels and forget that they are applying for the job of queen. The winning "look" should include personality, grace, and approachability. Your carriage will reflect your attitude of self from the inside out and that is something that is very difficult to conceal. I have watched too many contestants "wilt" before my very eyes when they are standing next to another contestant who they feel intimidated by either through beauty, height, or muscle tone. How you feel about yourself translates to how you carry yourself and working to develop yourself from the inside out will allow you to feel like the queen and convey the image even when standing next to who you may consider to be the most beautiful woman in the world!

Rhythm & Timing:

When walking in front of the judges during swimsuit or evening gown competition, you want to get your rhythm and timing down to where you are in control of your body and presentation rather than the music being in control of you! Practice training your body to do what you want it to do when you are calm and you will be able to control it when you are nervous!

Spin:

Modeling on the stage is like a presenting a silent movie, so you want to be as fluid and expressive as possible without appearing as if you are trying too hard. The more comfortable you are including spins while either walking down a long stage or spinning out of a pose, the more your judges and audience will enjoy your performance.

Transitions:

While executing your walk, spins, and poses you want to ensure to make the transition as fluid as possible so it appears natural rather than contrived. Practice your walk, your poses and your transitions in front of a mirror so you see what the judges see.

Understated:

There is something to be said about being the contestant who has a confident and slightly understated walk and presentation. By understated I do not mean to imply that you should pull your energy back while competing, rather use tension and movement to create grace on stage rather than looking like you are trying too hard. Everything is about attitude and movement, so record yourself walking and then ask yourself if you are conveying a presence of arrogance or confidence.

Value:

As the potential titleholder, contestants often view pageantry and being "judged" by a panel of five people in the sense of almost asking what value do you think I have in this pageant. If every contestant needs to believe they already have value and are just sharing it with the group of judges. Perception versus reality can be your best friend or your worst enemy when competing.

Walk:

Your walk is what helps separate you on stage from another contestant and can help you either win or lose the pageant. How graceful you are and how much personality you bring into your walk will help create the image of the complete package or just the contestant who is poised and pretty.

X- Factor!

What is that "it" factor -that intangible that makes a person take notice of a contestant when she walks into a room or onto the stage? Her confidence and stature on the stage is what draws the judge's eyes to these certain delegates.

Yourself:

Pageantry is a "me, myself, and I" sport and the only person who you are competing against on that stage is yourself. Value what you have to bring to the competition and try to not compare yourself to anyone else because there will always be somebody who is taller, prettier, smarter, and more graceful than ourselves. Guess what...the contestant who you think is that person is often comparing herself to another as well. You have to focus your energy and thoughts in the moment in order to give out the energy of charisma and enjoyment on that stage!

Zeal:

Your eagerness to accomplish a memorable performance onstage combined with your attitude and determination will ultimately help you win your next title. How you perform on the outside is dependent upon how much work you are willing to put forth to become that complete package and ultimately have a better appreciation for yourself and what you are capable of. Pageantry is a sport like many others that allows you to develop yourself from the inside out and allowing yourself to enjoy the journey is one of the greatest rewards you will ever receive!

Chapter 19

MENTAL CONDITIONING

I believe that 80% of winning comes from mental conditioning and not only did this apply to my national and international pageant wins, but I have met winners who have repeatedly mastered the art of mental conditioning. Before my win at the Ms. US Continental Pageant in 2000 and my win at Mrs. International in 2006, I developed my mental conditioning skills and visualized being on stage every night for 3 months. You could say that I literally lived and breathed those pageants before I even stepped foot on the stage, which I believe helped make my dreams a reality. I truly believe that the mental conditioning before a competition is as vital as the physical conditioning, because you have to *believe* that your goal is attainable, because what the mind believes - your reality conceives.

Those who know me well are aware of the fact that I am a very spiritual person. I believe that we are all created from energy and are continually creating our lives through conscious or unconscious thoughts, emotions, and actions. As a Reiki III Master, I have been trained and studied the mind/body connection and I used my tools to gain the competitive edge when I competed just as much as I utilized my tools of interview techniques, marketing skills, and presentation. In other words... in the pageants I won, I never left anything to chance and would control those things that I had control over and respected the processes that I didn't have control over. Pageant winners use this mental conditioning as a tool as do athletes and many people who excel in the world around you.

It has been proven repeatedly in sports training, and in quantum physics that the mind is the most powerful tool to create your life. So you can utilize this tool to either create your successes or your failures and either way, you are using your mind as a tool. Knowing this, wouldn't it be prudent to develop your mind skills to your advantage as well as your physical skills? You would not be any more willing to walk out on stage in a two-piece swimsuit without preparing physically and adopting a healthy diet, so why would you walk out on the stage or into an interview room without preparing mentally through every detail of the competition experience? Yet the majority of contestants when they compete, only focus on 50% of their competitive edge and literally leave the rest to chance.

Before I won some my biggest pageants, I *felt* different before I even stepped off of the plane to compete. There was a sense of peace and confidence that is indescribable to those who have never experienced it. When I coach my queen's I am told of the same feeling they had as we were working together or after the pageant is over. The element of knowing you are going to win the pageant comes from more than a superficial place of arrogance or insincere confidence, it stems from knowing when your hard work and your opportunity connect for the proper time to make your dreams a reality.

Mental conditioning can involve visualization, meditation, and various techniques that will assist you in not only presenting yourself as a stronger competitor, but allowing you to experience confidence throughout your pageant journey. As a contestant, I practiced visualization techniques every night before I competed and I teach all of my titleholders to do the same. I ask every one of my clients on their first session what their goal is for the pageant they are entering – after all, if I don't know what their goal is, then I can't help them achieve it. I have heard responses anywhere from the fact that they want to be in the top 10, the top 5, and some will be completely honest and tell me that their goal is to win.

Of course to all of the contestants who tell me that they will be happy just getting into the top 10 finalist position, my job is to ensure this is in fact what they truly desire. After all, if your goal is to make the top 10 finalist spot then I will work diligently to help you get there but I warn you…by the time you are in that position, it is too late to decide that you want to win the pageant now. Reason being that one contestant decided in *advance* that her goal was to win the pageant, and she worked diligently to perfect the extra details during her months of preparation to achieve this goal. By the time you are standing on stage next to her, she is already untouchable and we have all met that contestant. She is the one delegate who has the "it" factor and that intangible quality that is magnetizing, and draws your attention to her during the lineup. This is the contestant who decided months in advance that her goal was to win – and more often than not, she does.

What I have discovered is that so often we do not believe in our hearts that we have the ability to win the pageant, so rather than attempt to try and convince ourselves that we can win, we settle for telling ourselves that we just want to get into the top 10. Believe me I have been thrilled personally when I was able to get into the top 10 spot at my pageants, so I am not by any means negating the importance of being named a semi-finalist. What I want to ensure is that you set out to attain the actual goal you are trying to achieve, and not just settling for anything that you won't be personally satisfied with. Of course in any pageant you enter, there will be only one winner of the title, but if you allow yourself to dream big and do not limit yourself then you will be amazed at what you can accomplish! You push yourself to higher standards, break limiting beliefs, and ultimately remove yourself from the illusion that there was ever anything holding you back.

There is so much to pageantry that you can control and your mental conditioning allows you to feel more in control in an environment where it is very easy to lose focus and feel out of control. Remember my philosophy in life that you can control three things; your thoughts, your emotions, and your actions. Because the unknown factors are often what prevents us from either understanding what we are getting into or discerning what the job of titleholder requires, it becomes easier to remain in a state of naivety rather than seeking out the answers to these questions so you can feel more at ease. Again, I feel it comes down to the amount of belief that you have in yourself to achieve your goals.

In order for you as the contestant to feel as if the title is yours, you literally need to walk through the entire process of competition from entering the pageant, to winning, and finally to the execution of your role as titleholder. Get as many answers to as many questions can ask about the various systems, such as what is expected, and what role you should play in the process of queen. Not understanding what you are getting yourself into in the role of the titleholder, is similar to applying and interviewing for a job that you do not know what is expected. The element of the unknown is enough to throw the balance of your emotions off from your love to wanting to represent the pageant, to the fear of not knowing if you can do what is expected. Mental conditioning includes many elements of creating the vision in your mind of having this job so clear, that you can understand and ultimately *feel* what it is like to have this job before you even enter the judge's interview room. What your mind perceives to be real your actions will follow suit.

Educate Yourself:

Do your homework and ask former titleholders what was expected from them during their reign. Ask the directors of the system you enter what qualities her ideal titleholder should have. How often do they want to communicate with their queens and through what medium (email, phone calls, etc...) If the director is interested in making money for her system then find ways to help your director accomplish this goal. Directors spend countless hours and resources developing their systems because it is a business for them, and despite what we may think...their world does not revolve around us. This is a two-way partnership that allows the building of opportunities for the titleholder and the building of the business for the director which is why you need to work together. The more you know what your role would be as the titleholder, the more you can envision yourself performing the job.

Visualization:

If you have never visualized then you are going to enjoy how the power of the mind actually works in the creation of your dreams. Everything that you see in the world outside of you was first created in the world within someone's mind, and their thoughts, emotions, and actions are what created something from nothing. The most spectacular architecture, the most beautiful music, and the most inspired art all began as a vision, a thought, and through the creative detail of expression the thought became transformed in to something tangible. Turning an intangible into a tangible...that describes the process of pageantry and of attaining everything in life that your heart desires!

In the process of visualization, you want to create a picture in your mind so vivid that you cover all five senses to make it more realistic. When I visualized for months prior to winning my pageants, I visualized *feeling* heat of the spotlights on me, the *sound* of applause from the audience, the *touching* of the placement of the crown on my head, the *smell* of the roses that were handed to me and what the *look* on my husband's face would be when he walked out on stage to crown me. Every detail I covered every night for three months until I stood on that stage in Chicago and the feeling was similar to what I had envisioned...only better!

Practice your visualization techniques and as you progress, you will become more proficient at it and more aware of how you can create the details in your mind. You do not have to spend 30 minutes doing this, as I only spent approximately 10 minutes every night visualizing my win, but throughout the day when I was practicing my walk, my platform development, and my onstage interview, I was visualizing myself on that stage performing in the exact same manner as I did during the competition. Like everything that you will be perfecting in preparation for the pageant, visualization is about training your mind to create what you desire to experience in your reality.

Affirmations:

Daily affirmations play a vital role in negating the effects of fear-based thinking and self-limiting beliefs. They create a sense of awareness of what we are thinking and allow us to discover the root of the thought, which oftentimes was not even ours to begin with. By practicing your daily affirmations, which I suggest doing in the morning when you wake-up, then you can be more deliberate about how you create your life which transcends into how you compete. You will discover more and more, that among the beautiful women you share the stage with you are not competing against them, but rather *with* them. I like to get the neon colored index cards and write my affirmations on them so they are enjoyable to look at, and the vibrant colors intensify my emotions when I read my affirmations.

The best part about affirmations is that you can replace negative thinking with positive thoughts, which will build your self-esteem and confidence level. Listed are just some of my personal favorites, but you can tailor your own affirmations to meet your specific emotional and spiritual needs:

1. I am the new Mrs./Miss/Teen _____.

2. I can accomplish anything through my own efforts.

3. I control my own life through my thoughts, emotions, and actions.

4. The three most beautiful things about me are my:

    a. Smile

    b. Fitness

    c. Skin

5. I am confident, I am extraordinary, I am enough!

6. I don't need anyone's approval or permission to achieve my dreams!

7. I have the power to accomplish every goal I set before me.

8. I am smart, beautiful, and compassionate.

Whatever the negative thoughts and emotions are that you want to replace, ensure that you identify them and replace the negative thoughts with a positive affirmation. If you have always believed that you are not smart enough, then write down your positive affirmation that you are intelligent and wise. The purpose of your daily affirmations is to strengthen your confidence level and break down the barriers of illusion that you built to prevent achieving all of your goals. In order to become the queen, you need to *feel* like the winner from the inside out and that cannot be faked. It needs to be earned through recognition of your own greatness and acknowledging the amazing qualities that make you unique.

Meditation:

Meditating allows you alone time with self. In today's society we spend the majority of our time with others, and allow the voices of the world to often overpower our own inner voice. Meditating allows you to spend time alone with self and time alone with God. If you can shut off the voices of the world around you then you will know what you are thinking, feeling, and creating. Deliberate creation allows you to form your life from intention rather than spending 90% of your life on "auto pilot," and creating your life out of habit whether you like the results or not. The more comfortable you can become with yourself then you will be more comfortable in your own skin, which will translate into confidence both on and off the stage.

There are many different ways to meditate, so find a method that you are comfortable with and get into the daily habit of centering yourself, so during the pageant competition as well as throughout life you will feel more in control of your thoughts and feelings, which will lead you to control your actions.

Vision Board:

This is such a fun and unique way of creating the visual reminder of the goal you are attempting to attain. Remember that thoughts create your goals, so to constantly have a visual reminder of what you want to create helps you to remain focused on your goal. Vision boards allow you the freedom to use your imagination and focus through mental efforts on the goal you ultimately want to achieve. Now considering that I take into account thoughts, emotions and actions when trying to accomplish a goal then you have to go beyond just the visual when creating this.

First you should let your imagination run wild and allow yourself to dream big. When I coach contestants, I ask them the most important thing…"if you could accomplish anything with this title, what would it be?" Ask yourself this question when creating your vision board, then allow yourself the freedom to dream. Find magazines with pictures, words, and stories; anything that you connect with on a soul level and cut them out and past the onto your vision board. Use bright colors and anything that helps entice an emotion, so when you are pulling photos out of magazines and collecting those inspirational elements in which your mind will use to create – allow your heart and soul to aid you. Pull out the photos that when you are perusing through, draw a reaction from a soul level. Cut out those pictures that mesmerize you, and those will be the photos that will help you create your goal.

Chapter 20

THE WINNING ATTITUDE

Attitude is one of the most important elements to winning in pageantry and in life. The perspective you have towards yourself and the world around you will determine how hard you work towards achieving a goal, and much dedication and energy you will put into making your dream a reality. The difference between those contestants who pursue their goal until they accomplish their ultimate title and those who either quit reluctantly is often their attitude.

In order to develop your competitive skills to their highest level, you want to have an open mind and an expectant heart. With the combination of improving your mental conditioning, your interview skills, and your overall marketability, your open mind will allow you to reach beyond the limitations you have been experiencing and challenge yourself.

By also preparing for a competition with an open heart, you will also allow yourself to *feel* the dream and allow it to develop and flourish within your heart, and therefore connect with that place within your soul that allows you to enjoy the journey you are taking through pageantry. By opening your heart towards your platform, your passion, and your "why" you have the opportunity to not only help people that you share your message with, but you also have the chance to heal yourself through the power of your own message. Imagine overcoming your shyness, insecurities, and self-imposed limitations through your development. Pageantry allows you to challenge yourself and become greater than you have ever been on a physical, emotional, and spiritual level.

This is the attitude that winners possess before even stepping foot onto the competitive arena. They understand that through the development of their own unique strengths, they challenge themselves to greatness without even perceiving the contestants around them as competition. By the time a contestant believes she can win a pageant, she has not even met the judges, yet knows what message to convey in her interview and how she wants to translate that message. The winner has already established her strategy to separate herself from those around her by her image, platform, interview, presentation, and attitude. She will never be the contestant that is gossiping about others because she is too focused on her own goal to waste her time and energy on putting others down around her. The winner is the woman who looks at those around her as being a part of her journey towards the crown, and not an obstacle.

There are many strategies you can develop to help yourself attain a winning attitude, because like developing your competition strengths your attitude must also be developed to challenge you rather than work against you. Let's review some ways that you can maximize your positive attitude to feel and think like a winner.

Develop an "Attitude of Gratitude"

I believe the best form of gratitude you can experience is to count your blessings and then focus on the reasons to continue counting more. I have developed a habit, that when I wake up every morning before my feet even touch the floor I am saying a prayer of gratitude for my husband, my dogs, my health, and everything I can think of in those moments to be grateful for. I truly believe that if I live my life in an attitude of gratitude then I will discover more opportunities in my life to receive blessings. What you focus on continues to grow, whether your attention is creating positive or negative circumstances in your life.

Practice doing this every morning, and while preparing for your competition I would encourage you to discover more opportunities in which to be grateful. There are so many areas where you can be in an attitude of thankfulness and having the opportunity to spread your message, the right in this country as a woman to compete in a pageant, and the education you possess to be articulate enough to communicate your platform. If you are blessed enough to have the chance to compete in a pageant, then find reasons to be grateful and your experience will return to you more opportunities in which to be appreciative.

If you have a strong platform which has affected your life, then be grateful that you have healed enough to be able to share your message in hopes of inspiring and healing another who has experienced the same. If you have competition clothing that you wish was more expensive or flattering, then be grateful that you have the wardrobe now to compete in because many young women cannot afford to even own nice clothes. There are millions of opportunities throughout your life and your pageant journey in which to be grateful, so always have your attitude of gratitude and when you walk into the judge's interview room or onto the pageant stage, your attitude will be sincere, appreciative, and you will enjoy the journey so much more!

Come from a Place of Contribution

How often have you witnessed contestants who enter into a pageant with a "what is in it for me?" attitude? These contestants view the pageant as something that will benefit them, the directors and staff as individuals who are there to please them, and the opportunity as the titleholder being created to serve them. Nowhere in their perception of this journey have they realized that pageantry is in fact what you put into it, and if you fail to put energy, passion, and love into your title then you will certainly not be receiving it back. It' the law of life… you get what you give.

How can you as a contestant come from a place of giving rather than receiving? You create that sacred place where your heart, soul, and mind connect to strategically find areas within your journey to the crown that you may not have discovered an opportunity. One of the most obvious places begins with what you have to offer the pageant through the unique qualities and talents that you possess. If your goal is to maximize your talents of public speaking, then make a list of how you can benefit the pageant and your platform through public speaking opportunities. If you have the gift of developing relationships then use those abilities to develop relationships throughout your reign with potential sponsors of the pageant, and set a goal as to how many you would like to gain by the end of your reign.

Knowing what you want to offer the pageant rather than waiting to see what you can get out of the title will not only assist you in being a great titleholder, but you will be able to effectively communicate those abilities to the judges. The judge's interview room is where you as a contestant are able to express your motivations and your goals if you are selected as the queen. Knowing what your goals are in advance will assist you in clearly communicating them to the judge's panel in a short amount of time. Know your motivation and understand how you can bring benefit to the pageant and what legacy you can leave behind. I believe in anything that you do in life, try to leave it better than when you arrived and pageantry is no different. The partnership between pageants and the titleholders is one that should be respected enough to create an attitude of gratitude for the position you are in, whether you are a competitor or ultimately crowned the winner.

Before you sit down in front of a judge, come from a position of how you can leave the experience better than before you met. Rather than try to feed the judges what you think they want to hear, be prepared to provide something of contribution so by the end of the interaction, they will know something more about you and recognize your sincerity and compassion along with your obvious grace and beauty. Do you believe it is an accident that out of all the young women in your state, you were selected to represent your state or community? All of the years of pageant preparation and exhausting hours at the gym may have brought you to the final road in your journey, so share with even one judge how they can bring peace into their lives through something you shared about your platform. If pageantry is about making a difference in the lives of others, then never disregard the importance of the judges, directors, pageant staff, sponsors, or fellow contestants that were placed before you in your journey.

You may not realize that the judge you are speaking to just lost his daughter to breast cancer and something in your story will help them deal with the fear and the pain they are experiencing. The female judge who may have just lost her husband to heart disease or stroke, and the strength that you convey through your message and your passion to want to help others like her, may be something vital she needs in her grieving process.

Remember, that you are in a pageant because you want to experience a goal of making a difference and sharing an experience that has transformed your life, and will hopefully do the same for another. This is why it is so important to discover your "why" and realize that the goal you set before yourself to make a difference in the lives of others can be accomplished with or without the crown – depending on how you take advantage of the opportunities presented to you.

If you can speak to each and every judge with the sincerity and honesty that you speak to a group of cancer survivors, a room of children at a hospital, or a Senator who has the power to impact your state, every person you encounter throughout your pageant journey must be respected enough to understand that their connection to you even for a brief moment, could be the entire reason you were there as a contestant in the system. If you understand this, then you realize the power you have to make a difference, and your attitude in the interview room and throughout the pageant will be from "need" to "want." The interaction will feel less like desperation and you will appear more confident in front of the judges when you come from a place of contribution.

Realize that You Cannot Fail

One of the most important lessons that you can learn throughout your journey to the crown is that pageantry is a part of your journey, it is not the destination. When I competed in pageants, my goal was never to just to win a crown and banner, but to be the contestant who could inspire another to believe in the power of their dreams. When I became a pageant coach, my goal each and every day is to help inspire another to believe in the power of their dreams, and as an author my goal remains the same…to inspire another to believe in the power of their dreams. Knowing what my intention is before I enter into any endeavor allows me the ability to focus on creating my ultimate goal, and as a contestant you also have the ability to do the same.

Before your competition and prior to even selecting your wardrobe, it is vital to understand your "why" and ultimately what you want to achieve by competing in your selected pageant. Knowing that a crown and banner does not define you any more than a car, clothing or your friends, you have to be cognizant of what your ultimate goal is through competing in pageantry. Dig below the surface and the superficial answers of "world peace" and discover what you want to achieve, and that is the goal you must set out to accomplish. From there, you can realize your goal with or without the crown, and if you do win the title then you have discovered a new venue in which to continue pursuing your goal.

Write your goal down on a brightly colored index card and place it on your vanity mirror, next to your work station, and anywhere that you can remind yourself of what you desire to accomplish. This is the ultimate goal of competing in pageantry because so much of competition is about perfecting the details and then leaving the rest to God. By realizing that your ultimate goal is something you alone have the power and control to achieve, then you feel more empowered during your preparations and especially when you are standing on the stage and shining your light from the inside out.

Your goal is your ultimate crown and by knowing that you can achieve it with or without the judge's permission or approval, then you have just won the ultimate "crown" in your pageant. This is controllable so place as much energy in the creation of your goal as you are in your preparation in the gym, on the stage, and in the judge's interview room. By doing this, you will enter any pageant journey with a winning attitude and with or without the crown, know that you are in control of your journey and can challenge yourself and release yourself from any self-imposed barriers.

Define Yourself – Define the Crown

Throughout the journey of competition, it becomes so easy to lose yourself in the preparation of the competition if you have not already defined yourself from your image, platform, and your presentation. While preparing with your team of designers, make-up artists, coaches, and directors, you run the risk of presenting represent. All too often I have spoken to contestants who have changed their platforms, hair color, sense of style, and everything they stood for because they allowed the voices of their team become louder than their own voice. The most important piece of advice I can offer you is to never lose yourself in the competition. You define the crown and it is your job to redefine beauty and the look of the titleholder every year – not imitate it. Honor your look and trust yourself and your own ability to be enough. You do not have to be a cookie cutter imitation of a previous queen in order to excel in pageantry; you must just be true to yourself and feel confident enough in your own skin to be able to convey to the judges that you are the person for the job.

How do you define the crown? You do this with every possible opportunity whether it is in the judge's interview room, during pageant week when photographers are shooting your photos, or on the stage with the other contestants. When I competed for the Mrs. International Pageant, my goal was to stand out among the amazing group of women I shared the stage with by focusing on my unique look, and my ability to market myself from my 16 years of experience in radio sales. I wanted to redefine the look of a queen by competing in straight, long hair with a more "model" look that represented who I was rather than attempting to change my personal style. My entire life I have been told by complete strangers that I looked like a model, so I used that image to set myself apart from the rest.

Oftentimes the problem arises when contestants attempt to second guess a judge and try to become the version of themselves they believe the judges want to see. The judges actually want to see the best version of *you*, and you do such a disservice to yourself when you do not believe in the woman that you have become enough to celebrate your own sense of self. When I judged pageants from state to international, I heard the same phrases uttered by judges, and this was that each judge just wants one contestant to be comfortable enough to let the judges know she is the *one*. There are so many ways of accomplishing this task without losing yourself in the process.

That crown is nothing more than a beautiful piece adornment without a contestant who gives it meaning. Your purpose, integrity, character, and all of those amazing qualities that define you…is what ultimately defines the crown. Yet so often during one's quest for the coveted title, contestants lose their sense of identity and rather than allowing the crown to become a representation of them, they attempt to become the crown. You are far too valuable to ever diminish yourself to the level of being identified by a material ornament.

Discover the assets that you celebrate and use those to set yourself apart. When you set out to accomplish your ultimate goal in pageantry, you will realize that the crown is what you define it to be. You can create it to represent empowerment for women with breast cancer, education for adults suffering from heart disease, or awareness and support for those who are afflicted with Alzheimer's disease. As the titleholder, you have the opportunity in many systems to be your own marketing genius, advocate, and role model, so choose your system carefully and respect your motivation to be true to yourself and define your title.

Decide in advance what it is that you want to accomplish and set your goals step by step so the journey feels tangible to you. Unless you believe in advance that you can win the pageant, so by the time you arrive at competition it is too late to convince yourself that this goal is attainable. Define the title prior to your arrival and how you can come from a place of contribution. Decide how you want to inspire another through your journey and you will ultimately transform yourself to be the queen that you are attempting to become. Step by step you will think like a winner, feel like a winner and act like a winner who has the confidence and ease to compete among her group of sisters without arrogance, fear, or insecurity.

Breaking the Habit

Every contestant who has ever been coached by me has heard my "mantra" repeatedly to the point they can say it in their sleep. My mantra is this… "You have to become comfortable…being *uncomfortable*." We are all creatures of habit, and as such, we are very comfortable setting our thoughts, emotions, and actions on autopilot. We *think* the same each and every day which leads to *feel* the same emotions, which causes us to perform the same *actions*, and ultimately we experience the same results. Yet, contestants all too often after they do not win a pageant will sit back, scratch their head, and wonder why they had the same result in pageants. The reason is this…you failed to change the important competitive factors and instead, you decided to change the superficial elements which begin and end with which all too often include your evening gown, your photos, or your platform. Those are all the superficial elements factored into competing in a pageant, but they are the easiest to control and the most enjoyable to prepare for. I love clothing as much as the next contestant, to the point where I earned my Bachelor's Degree with an emphasis in Fashion Merchandising and Design. That being said, if I had just changed my wardrobe when I competed in pageants without actually changing my strategy, then I would have experienced the same results in a different gown. In order to have a different result as a contestant, you have to change something in your pattern of behavior. Period!

I expect every contestant that I work with to ask me what my strategy is to help them win. As a coach, if I am not asked this question, then I assume that the contestant has not yet developed into the top notch competitor that she needs to become in order to win a pageant – which is why she has sought me out to help her. Neglecting to ask your trainer what their strategy is to accomplish your goal of winning is similar to failing to ask your accountant how they will prepare your taxes, your teacher how they will educate your child, and your partner how they will help your relationship grow. Pageant coaches are designed to assist you in developing your greatest strengths into your competitive advantage and your perceived weaknesses into your secret weapon.

Get comfortable being uncomfortable and challenge yourself on a mind, body, and soul level to step outside of the "box" and realize that you already are the titleholder you dream of becoming. The only difference is that you have not yet accepted it due to limiting thoughts and beliefs, so break the habit of being comfortable in accepting fear and self-denial, and see yourself for the amazing competitor you already are. If you continue looking outside of yourself for the competition, then there are many avenues that you can use to continue seeing pageantry as something outside of yourself. In fact, pageantry is the just the opposite – it is a vehicle that allows you to see yourself through your greatest strengths and encourages you to strengthen those areas of your life where you feel you need an additional "push."

In fact, in any area of your life where you feel that you are putting forth a concerted amount of effort and are not seeing the results that you wish to see, examine what you are doing out of habit and what you are deliberately challenging yourself with to become better than you were before.

Beyond the Crown

Chapter 21

AFTER THE PAGEANT...

There is no age limit for achieving your dreams, so if you have the moment of today to think about what you want to become then you have this moment to achieve your goal, and you do not need the permission or the approval of another person to achieve that goal. Pageantry is about the sisterhood of dreamers who all share the stage to learn self-love, self-acceptance, and ultimately self-sufficiency. Become your greatest advocate and your own best friend, and realize that your journey is far greater than winning a crown and banner. It is about being allowed to dissolve your own self-imposed barriers, and break down your illusion of fear that has kept you paralyzed from achieving your own greatness. Pageantry has always been about you becoming the greatest version of *yourself*, and in that process, learning to love and respect yourself as you do others. Pageantry is about you finally coming to the realization that you *are* the queen you have been trying to become.

When you accomplish the development of every area of your competitive skills, you will realize that there is nothing you cannot do. From this moment on, look at the crown as a goal to accomplish what your crown ultimately *represents* to you. If the title you are striving to achieve is to heal yourself from an old "illusion" or break down old self-imposed barriers, then let that objective be your primary goal. So when you are standing on that stage and shining your light, you will see that you are the representation of the queen you have always wanted to become.

I remember when I began competing in pageants, I had suffered from such lack of self-esteem that I truly felt I had only ladders to climb from what my perception of myself was. In other words, I could not feel any worse about myself than I already had, so the judge's opinion of me could not be any more critical than my own opinion of myself was. While I competed, I learned to set certain goals in each pageant that I entered, and if that goal was an internal step beyond my comfort zone, or an external drive to help other women educate themselves about breast cancer, then my goal was always beyond the crown. It represented a part of my healing that I would someday realize was within my ability to heal throughout my entire pageant journey.

I hope that you realize that through your journey in life, just as in your journey through pageantry, you hold the key to transform yourself into anything you wish to become. Just enjoy the process and don't take it all so seriously, because every moment of your life you get the chance to make your dreams come true.

If you asked a panel of five judges for permission to represent your local, state, national, or international title and these five individuals said "no," then my philosophy is that you need to ask another group of five strangers, and continue searching until you have perfected your competitive game to finally get a "yes." Much like life, pageantry is not about seeking the approval from people to achieve your dreams rather it is about seeking the approval from yourself to continue striving towards your ultimate goal. Do not stop attempting to reach your dream until you feel you have literally exhausted every possibility and then, just when you are ready to give up, try one more time. I cannot count the number of stories from women who have overcome obstacles and reached their goals in pageantry just through sheer determination, and you are reading the words from somebody who has done just that!

Prior to winning my national pageant in 2000, I literally had a woman tell me that it was time to hang up my pageant heels and "get a life." She thought she was coming from a place of contribution, but something told me that she was the type of person who had continually given up on her own dreams prior to ever reaching them. Although her comments truly upset me, I cried for two hours then wiped the tears from my face and began strategizing as to how I would come back the next time and win the pageant… and I did win it one year later! Be very cautious as to who you take advice from, because if the person you are taking advice from is not coming from a place of contribution or has not achieved the level of success that you desire to accomplish, then you risk becoming exactly like them.

Pageantry is a journey - not a destination. My hope is that somewhere in the pages of this book, you have discovered a part of your own voice that you may not have heard once before. Learn to trust that voice before you trust the voices of the world around you, and realize that the person you may be called to make a difference in the life of....just may be yourself. Throughout my childhood years, I struggled with self-esteem issues because I was not exactly what you would have considered pretty. I tell people that I know God has an amazing sense of humor, and if you don't believe me, then I could show you some pictures of me as a child! Pageantry was a journey that allowed me to embrace my uniqueness and celebrate my passions through a venue that I could enjoy. It taught me that the perception of the world outside of me was not what mattered most, rather my perception of self that was relevant. The journey through pageantry allowed me to realize that with any goal, it begins and ends with me and not with a group of judges. If I could identify my own purpose prior to ever stepping foot on a stage, then I could control my ultimate outcome – with or without the crown.

Being in such a competitive arena allowed me to silence the voices of those around me who wanted to share their fear and anxiety, and tune in to my own inner voice that echoed truth. My journey through pageantry was about developing my skills to the level where I could help another woman realize the power she has to make any of her dreams come true. I suppose you could say that my greatest accomplishment in pageantry was helping others realize their own magnificence, and understand that you are all the epitome of the beauty queens you are trying to become. You define the crown, and *you* give it meaning. Without your passion and love for what you do and who you are, the crown would be just a piece of metal sitting on a shelf.

Your soul breathes life into this object and allows it to represent what matters most to you, so do not ever forget that without you – the crown is still just a crown. Create your dreams one thought at a time, and through the process, allow yourself to inspire another to become their own personal best.

This book was in part to honor my mother, who taught me that we all have the ability to turn our most painful experiences, into our greatest achievements. Although I will never get another chance to say good-bye, I believe that she is around me, watching over me, and encouraging me to continue reaching for my dreams. My encouragement to you is the same – never, never, never give up on your dreams! You alone own the power to create your life exactly as you want to experience it. You have the ability each and every day to define yourself through your thoughts, emotions, and actions. Sometimes the one that makes the biggest difference is not the person who is screaming from the top of the mountain, but the one who flutters her wings and creates a ripple effect across the world, one person at a time.

Our ripple effects are often created from the choices that we make whether we ever get a second chance at them or not. It's about the joy in life that keeps bringing us back to a place of healing, and at the crossroads or at the stage where the healing takes place, you can finally spread your wings and fly. During some of the lowest points in my life when certain situations didn't make sense, my mom would always smile and give me a reassuring look. She would explain to me that life was about transformations, and sometimes the most profound transformations would be the most painful and often take the longest amount of time to develop. For many years, mom would always tell me that I was a caterpillar in the "cocoon stage" and one day, when I least expected it, I would realize that I had transformed into a butterfly. Well momma, I think I have finally become that butterfly.

> *"Just when the caterpillar thought the world was over, it became a butterfly."*
>
> *Proverb*

Chapter 22

BREAST CANCER AWARENESS

Many of us know of someone who is either battling cancer or has at some point had to fight this disease. Although there is no known cause for breast cancer, being knowledgeable and proactive may one day save your life or the life of another that you help educate.

It is recommended that you:

- Understand your risks through family history or discussing it with a medical doctor.
- Begin getting your screenings such as mammograms and clinical breast exams.
- Understand and know your body so you are aware of any breast changes.
- Make healthy lifestyle choices which include eating well and getting constant exercise.

With so many advances in the medical field, breast cancer is being detected early which allows more women to survive this disease. Education is the key! Visit the Susan G. Komen, American Cancer Society, or the National Breast Cancer Foundation websites for more information.

FOR MORE INFORMATION

For more information on Creating Queens™ Pageant Coaching, Workshops, or Motivational Speaking Events in your area, please contact Suzy Bootz at:

For more Creating Queens™ books series:
Website: www.suzybootz.com
Email: suzy@suzybootz.com

Follow me on Twitter! - @suzy_bootz
Facebook: Suzy Bootz
Instagram: @realsuzybootz

Other Books by Suzy Bootz

Through the Eyes of Truth – A Conversation with God about My Life, Your Life, and Discovering Our Purpose – Available in Kindle, Audio, and Print on Amazon

Living, Dying, and the Seasons of Change – Available in Kindle and Print on Amazon

Heaven Scent – Love Letters from Beyond: Available in Kindle and Print on Amazon

Creating Utopia: Available in Kindle and Print on Amazon

Creating Queens – Secrets in Pageantry: Available in Kindle and Print on Amazon

To live inspired please visit www.suzybootz.com or www.throughtheeyesoftruth.com.

www.ingramcontent.com/pod-product-compliance
Lightning Source LLC
Chambersburg PA
CBHW070916180426
43192CB00037B/1424